THE ART OF WOODWORKING

BUILDING
CHAIRS

THE ART OF WOODWORKING

BUILDING CHAIRS

TIME-LIFE BOOKS
ALEXANDRIA, VIRGINIA

ST. REMY PRESS
MONTREAL • NEW YORK

THE ART OF WOODWORKING was produced by
ST. REMY PRESS

PUBLISHER	Kenneth Winchester
PRESIDENT	Pierre Léveillé
Series Editor	Pierre Home-Douglas
Series Art Director	Francine Lemieux
Senior Editor	Marc Cassini
Editor	Jim McRae
Art Directors	Normand Boudreault, Luc Germain
Designers	François Daxhelet, Hélène Dion, Jean-Guy Doiron, Michel Giguère
Picture Editor	Christopher Jackson
Writers	Andrew Jones, David Simon
Research Assistant	Bryan Quinn
Contributing Illustrators	Gilles Beauchemin, Roland Bergerat, Michel Blais, Ronald Durepos, James Thérien
Administrator	Natalie Watanabe
Production Manager	Michelle Turbide
System Coordinator	Jean-Luc Roy
Photographer	Robert Chartier
Administrative Assistant	Dominique Gagné
Indexer	Christine M. Jacobs

Time-Life Books is a division of Time Life Inc.,
a wholly owned subsidary of
THE TIME INC. BOOK COMPANY

TIME-LIFE INC.

President and CEO	John M. Fahey
Editor-in-Chief	John L. Papanek

TIME-LIFE BOOKS

President	John D. Hall
Vice-President, Director of Marketing	Nancy K. Jones
Managing Editor	Roberta Conlan
Director of Design	Michael Hentges
Director of Editorial Operations	Ellen Robling
Consulting Editor	John R. Sullivan
Vice-President, Book Production	Marjann Caldwell
Production Manager	Marlene Zack
Quality Assurance Manager	James King

THE CONSULTANTS

Mike Dunbar builds fine furniture at his workshop in Portsmouth, New Hampshire. The author of seven books and a contributing editor of *American Woodworker* and *Early American Life* magazines, Dunbar also offers Windsor chairmaking seminars across North America.

Giles Miller-Mead taught advanced cabinetmaking at Montreal technical schools for more than ten years. A native of New Zealand, he has worked as a restorer of antique furniture.

Building chairs.
    p. cm.— (The Art of woodworking)
  Includes index.
  ISBN 0-8094-9525-2
  1. Chairs.
  2. Furniture making. I. Time-Life Books.
II. Title: Building chairs.
III. Series.
TT197.5.C45B85 1994
  684.1'3—dc20   94-30363
                                      CIP

For information about any Time-Life book,
please call 1-800-621-7026, or write:
Reader Information
Time-Life Customer Service
P.O. Box C-32068
Richmond, Virginia
23261-2068

CONTENTS

Sam Maloof on
DESIGNING CHAIRS

I have designed more than 500 pieces of furniture in nearly 50 years of working wood. I have done furniture for homes, offices, churches, and schools, although I prefer designing for homes. Even now I take time to design and make at least five new pieces a year no matter how busy I am or how far behind I am in filling orders.

I do many drawings of pieces that come to mind but I also have hundreds more stored away mentally. I make drawings of case goods and tables for my clients, but chairs are designed as I make the prototype. I was asked some time ago to submit a drawing of a chair with dimensions for a publication. Because I did not have a drawing at hand I had to take measurements from a chair in our home.

When making a chair, I don't follow any formula or template; each chair is slightly different. I like to use my own body as a pattern. I cut out spindles for my rocking chair on a bandsaw by eye, and then hold the spindle to my back in a sitting position. If it feels good, I have a pattern. So far, the chairs that come out of my shop seem to fit the users.

I believe my furniture is functional and for everyday use; I want every piece I make to be useful to the person who buys it. In a rocking chair, I like to shoot for a rocker that doesn't tip too far back or pitch you forward. But I also want all of my chairs to be beautifully made. For instance, the joinery is always exposed. Why hide a beautifully made joint? When laying out legs for my rocking chair, I like to look for grain that follows the curve of the leg. A chair should invite a person to be seated, to embrace that person and make them comfortable. I want him or her to touch and feel the warmth and sensuousness of the wood, to relax.

I believe any person in the arts—in whatever medium—has a responsibility to share with others whatever knowledge he may have learned, something I have been able to do in my workshops. I always tell my students: No matter how beautiful the wood or how well made the chair, if it does not sit well it isn't a good chair. I like to think that my chairs sit very well.

Sam Maloof designs and builds fine furniture in his Alta Loma, California, workshop. He was the first woodworker ever elected a Fellow of the American Craft Council, and his chairs are in the permanent collection of the Museum of Fine Arts in Boston. He is the author of Sam Maloof: Woodworker, *published by Kodansha International Books.*

Arthur Mitchell talks about the
CHALLENGE OF CHAIRS

Over the years I have built all types of wooden furniture pieces, from stands to cabinets, desks to tables, and case goods to grandfather clocks. Yet to me, the ultimate challenge for a woodworker is to design and build a chair. If you accept the "challenge of the chair," first acquaint yourself with the standard dimensions and angles that are involved. Examine various chair styles, ranging from the simple to the ornate, then select a look that is personally pleasing and incorporate your own ideas. If you do not have the confidence to create a design yourself, choose a ready-made plan and start building.

The design phase can be as hard as the actual construction of the chair. A metamorphosis almost always happens between an idea and the finished, final piece. I have found that it is very rare to create an original design that does not require change. Sometimes it is even necessary to make several prototypes before building the actual chair. Even the smallest adjustment to size or the location of key parts can greatly enhance a chair's appeal.

In the construction of my chairs I strive for a design that will have broad appeal while withstanding the stresses of daily use. Proven joinery techniques are essential. Chairs are subjected to a variety of stresses; wood expands and contracts with humidity. Most of the chairs I produce use a leg that passes through the seat, which is then glued and wedged in place. The direction of the wood grain of the leg is oriented with that of the seat. To strengthen the legs I use either a brace that is screwed to the leg and chair bottom or traditional stretchers. The same pass-through technique incorporating a wedge is used wherever possible, especially with spindles that support the arms of a chair and also on some styles where the spindles are attached to the crest rail. Dowel pins are also used in strategic places to ensure that parts cannot separate.

Although I have always favored a traditional approach to woodworking design and construction techniques, I feel drawn towards experimentation. It was this desire to do something different with chair design, combined with a streak of pragmatism, that gave rise to my Sunburst Windsor armchair, like the one shown in the photograph at right. The chair features a removable top that could be finished separately. My other chairs also feature plain, straight lines or smooth, flowing curves that are free of ornament.

A well-designed chair is a thing of beauty and functionality. Built properly, it will last for generations. Don't hesitate to take up the challenge of making your own.

Arthur Mitchell designs and builds chairs in his workshop in Temple, Maine. Mitchell began making furniture at the age of 12. He has also worked as a builder and designer of fine-quality homes.

Carolyn and John Grew-Sheridan on their
FITTING CHAIR

Designing and building chairs is somewhat like writing. Whether you are producing a simple stool or an ornate dining chair—a short poem or a complex novel—each project has its own form, intent, and inherent challenges, as well as personal, social, and cultural meaning. This range of possibilities is what makes chair design so challenging and appealing.

Since training at Peters Valley Crafts Center in Layton, New Jersey, 20 years ago, we have developed nearly two dozen chair designs for limited production and custom orders. All have benefitted from our first chair, made from recycled oak barn wood, with a simple canvas seat and back. The item was supposed to be the ultimate in inexpensive, comfortable seating.

The first person to sit in this chair was Mary Coes, the diminutive adult daughter of our friends Vinton and Eleanor Coes. She nearly disappeared in our first masterpiece, designed for "every-person." Her generous comment was that experiencing our chair was like sitting in her grandfather's lap. From that first humbling review, we have been reminded continually that chair making is a reconciliation of esthetic, functional, technical, and personal requirements, full of compromises.

There is no such thing as a standard chair. The seat height of a dining chair, for example, can range from 13 ½ to 20 ½ inches. Chairs can be used for any number of activities, from reading and relaxing to talking and dining. Some chairs are built solely for ceremonial occasions, others to alleviate the distress of physical disabilities. Consequently, it can be helpful to have a convenient and reliable technique for measuring the physical form of a chair's user and experimenting with their personal preferences. We use our adjustable measuring chair, shown in the photo at left and on page 13, to supplement other traditional design tools, such as drawing models and prototypes.

Whether a customer is tall or short, wide or narrow, long or short of thigh or calf, we can easily investigate different options and combinations for a chair's dimensions and angles. The rig features five back supports, and adjustments for the height and angle of the seat and the arm rest. By moving the supports up or down, or in or out, we can fine tune the rig until we have the best "fit" for the sitter. Using graph paper or a computer, the settings are then plotted, creating a side view of the chair. That forms the basis of a three-dimensional view from which we can then fashion a full-size mock-up using corrugated cardboard.

But the fitting chair is only a beginning. The outline the rig provides is like the outline of a story. It's a skeleton upon which you can build everything that you want to embody in the chair's style, using, meaning, and emotional content.

Carolyn and John Grew-Sheridan build custom-fitted
chairs in their studio in San Francisco, California.

CHAIR-BUILDING BASICS

For millenia, chairs have been expected to exceed the seemingly simple demands of seating. Comfort, durability, and beauty are the criteria they must meet. The best provide a seamless blend of all three qualities. The worst can be bad indeed. Well-designed and properly built chairs provide comfortable and durable seating, are pleasing to look at, and fit into their surroundings. Small wonder that chair making is often considered to be the pinnacle of the woodworker's art.

By the time their use became more widespread in Europe in the 16th Century, chairs had become stylized to serve specific purposes. Dining chairs were built to fit around dining tables, and writing chairs were often paired with desks. Often, neither was matched to the human form; comfort frequently took second place to the formal function. Traditional dining chairs, for example, feature a backrest at an almost 90° angle to the seat, obliging the user to sit ramrod straight.

Although function remains an important design consideration, chair makers today typically give first consideration to

The adjustable chair-fitting jig shown above, designed by San Francisco furniture makers Carolyn and John Grew-Sheridan, takes the guesswork out of making comfortable, ergonomically sound chairs that are tailor-made to the user's body and posture. For more information on the device and on custom-fitting a chair, see pages 11 and 15.

the human form in their work, particularly when they are building custom-made chairs. The jig shown at left allows a chair to fit as snugly as a comfortable pair of shoes. The charts and illustrations on pages 14 and 15 will help you reconcile the sometimes conflicting demands of function and human anatomy in your designs, allowing you to build chairs that are both useful and comfortable.

Once you have designed a comfortable chair, it is time to turn your attention to appearance. A visual gallery of the most popular and enduring chair styles, from the Greek *Klismos* of the 5th Century BC—an armless chair that Homer said was favored by the goddesses—to Sam Maloof's classic modern rocking chair, is presented starting on page 18. As the examples show, the design possibilities for chair making are virtually limitless.

The information on pages 16 and 17 will help you in one of the more ordinary, but crucial, aspects of chair making: selecting the appropriate woods for your projects and determining how much lumber you need.

First made in late 17th-Century England, the Windsor chair is one of the most enduring and popular of all chair designs. Today, its precise joinery and functional elegance harken back to the craftsmanship of a bygone era. Many of the elements of the comb-back Windsor shown at left—the legs, spindles, stretcher, rungs, and arm bow—were riven and shaped from green wood. The chair was made by North Carolina woodworker Drew Langsner.

DESIGNING A COMFORTABLE CHAIR

Most people rate comfort as the most important requirement of a chair. Style, appearance, and sturdy joinery are also undeniable key elements, but if any of these criteria results in an uncomfortable chair, the product may end up being used as little more than an attractive showpiece.

Uncomfortable chairs give rise to a familiar litany of complaints: cutting off circulation to the legs; straining neck, shoulder, and back muscles; and squeezing the legs together. Each of these problems stems from the fact that, although very few people share the same size and shape, most chair designs are inspired by the "one size fits all" philosophy. Some chairs, like those found in fast-food restaurants for example, are actually intended to be uncomfortable to discourage users from sitting in them for lengthy periods.

The standard dimensions for various types of chairs presented in the chart below derive from the statistical sciences of anthropometry and ergonomics, which deal with measuring human bodies and tailoring what is made to the human form. The measurements provide good starting points for designing chairs, but following these guidelines slavishly will yield pieces that are only well suited for people of average build. Standard-size chairs can be uncomfortable for individuals who do not fit the mold: children; pregnant women; or people who are taller, shorter, or heavier than the average. But as a woodworker, you have the opportunity to fine-tune the design of your chairs to fit the individual user.

There are a few basic principles to follow. Seats that slope back slightly, for example, help position body weight more comfortably. Positioning a seat so that the user's feet will be firmly planted on the floor will not cut off circulation to the legs. Armrests that are properly located will minimize muscle tension in the shoulders. If the whole chair is to be angled back, the seat must also tilt backward to keep the user from sliding forward and prevent the front of the seat from cutting off circulation to the legs.

Well-designed backrests that conform to the shape of the human spine are crucial. For instance, a backrest should be concave to wrap around the back of the rib cage, shoulders, and waist. It should also curve from bottom to top, rather than be made perfectly straight, in order to support the vertebrae forming the reverse curve of the spinal column. Whatever its style, function, or design, a chair must support the lower five vertebrae in the small of the back, known as the lumbar region. And for a reclining chair, which places the head behind the center of gravity, the backrest must be high enough to also support the spine's upper section, known as the dorsal region.

STANDARD CHAIR DIMENSIONS

TYPE OF CHAIR	SEAT WIDTH	SEAT DEPTH	SEAT HEIGHT	BACK HEIGHT	SEAT ANGLE FROM HORIZONTAL	BACKREST ANGLE FROM VERTICAL
Arm Dining	20" to 24"	16" to 20"	17" to 18 ½"	40" to 48"	0°	5° to 10°
Side Dining	18" to 21"	16" to 20"	17" to 18 ½"	40" to 48"	0°	5° to 10°
Kitchen	14" to 16"	14" to 16"	17" to 18 ½"	30" to 36"	0° to 5°	5° to 10°
Desk chair	18" to 20"	16"	17" to 18 ½"	36" to 42"	0° to 5°	5° to 10°
Counter stool	16" to 18"	16" to 18"	Up to 30" (foot rest 20" below seat)	36" to 42"	0° to 5°	5° to 10°
Rocking chair	18" to 22"	16" to 20"	16" to 17"	36" to 42"	5° to 10°	20° to 25°
Lounging	22"	17"	24"	33"	10°	30° to 40°
High chair	12" to 14"	12" to 14"	22" to 28"	36" to 40"	0°	0° to 5°
Upholstered sofa	24" per person	18" to 22"	15 ½"	34" to 36"	5° to 15°	25°

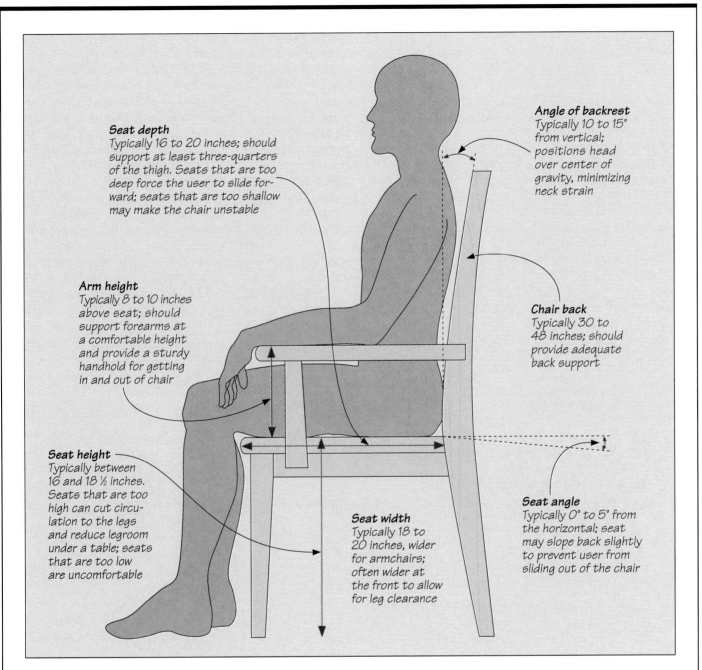

Seat depth
Typically 16 to 20 inches; should support at least three-quarters of the thigh. Seats that are too deep force the user to slide forward; seats that are too shallow may make the chair unstable

Angle of backrest
Typically 10 to 15° from vertical; positions head over center of gravity, minimizing neck strain

Arm height
Typically 8 to 10 inches above seat; should support forearms at a comfortable height and provide a sturdy handhold for getting in and out of chair

Chair back
Typically 30 to 48 inches; should provide adequate back support

Seat height
Typically between 16 and 18 ½ inches. Seats that are too high can cut circulation to the legs and reduce legroom under a table; seats that are too low are uncomfortable

Seat width
Typically 18 to 20 inches, wider for armchairs; often wider at the front to allow for leg clearance

Seat angle
Typically 0° to 5° from the horizontal; seat may slope back slightly to prevent user from sliding out of the chair

CUSTOM-FITTING A CHAIR

Like a tailored suit, a custom-built chair should be made to follow the contours of a particular user's body. To design such a chair, have the person sit upright on a flat bench and take the measurements listed at right. Using your measurements along with the anatomy illustration shown above and the standard dimensions in the chart on page 14, you can make a mockup chair from a light material like corrugated cardboard, laminated to whatever thickness of stock you need with thinned white glue. This mockup can help you design the chair and make the templates you will need to size its parts.

- For seat width, measure across the hips.
- For seat height, measure from the floor to the underside of the user's knee.
- For maximum seat depth, measure from the crook of the knee to the lower back.
- For arm rest height, measure from the seat to the elbow.
- To determine where lumbar support is needed, measure from the seat to the waist.
- For minimum backrest height for a dining chair, measure from the seat to the armpit.

SELECTING AND ORDERING WOOD

While a chair can be made from virtually any species of wood, there are advantages to choosing strong, dense hardwoods. Such woods will resist the stress and abuse that chairs must typically endure. A chair need not necessarily be built from a single species, however, particularly if it will be painted or if the visual effect of contrasting woods is not too jarring.

Your local lumberyard is an obvious source of wood, and often the most convenient. But selection may be limited to construction woods such as pine, spruce, and other softwoods. Although you may find the occasional cache of hardwood, more often than not you will have to venture farther afield, consulting the Yellow Pages or woodworking magazines to find lumber dealers who specialize in some of the less common hardwoods used for fine furniture. You will usually pay more, but the quality of the wood will be higher too.

There are other less costly options for finding the wood you need. A lumber mill may sell you boards at a reasonable price, but most often the wood will need to be seasoned and surfaced, which means that you must have access to a jointer and a thickness planer. Salvaged wood is relatively inexpensive and, because it often comes from old-growth timber, it can be visually and structurally superior to recently harvested lumber. And if you can fell your own trees or obtain some recently felled stock, green wood is ideal for some chairs.

Regardless of your chosen supply, define your needs carefully before ordering your wood. When calculating how much lumber you need, make a detailed cutting list of the finished pieces of lumber needed for a particular chair *(page 27 for frame chairs; page 53 for slab-and-stick chairs).*

Use the formula shown below to determine how many board feet you may need, and add 20 to 40 per cent (depending on the grade) to account for inevitable waste and defects in the wood. Because some chairs feature many curved parts, the degree of waste can run 50 percent or higher. The tips that follow

CALCULATING BOARD FEET

Ordering lumber by the board foot
The "board foot" is a unit of measurement used to calculate the volume of a given amount of stock. It is commonly used with hardwood lumber. As shown in the illustration at right, the standard board foot is equivalent to a piece that is 1 inch thick, 12 inches wide, and 12 inches long. To calculate the number of board feet in a piece of wood, multiply its three dimensions together. Then, divide the result by 144 if the dimensions are in inches, or by 12 if just one dimension is in feet.

The formula for a standard board:
1" x 12" x 12" ÷ 144 = 1
(or 1" x 12" x 1' ÷ 12 = 1)
So, if you had a 6-foot-long plank that is 1 inch thick and 4 inches wide, you would calculate the board feet as follows: 1" x 4" x 6' ÷ 12 = 2 (or 2 board feet). Other examples are shown in the illustration. Remember that board feet are calculated on the basis of the nominal rather than actual dimensions of the stock; consequently, the board feet contained in a 2-by-4 that actually measures 1½-by-3½ inches would be calculated using the larger dimensions.

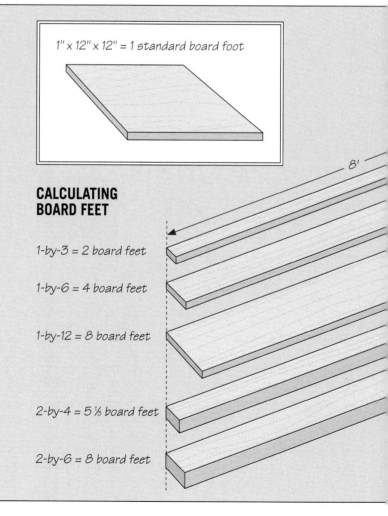

1" x 12" x 12" = 1 standard board foot

CALCULATING BOARD FEET

1-by-3 = 2 board feet

1-by-6 = 4 board feet

1-by-12 = 8 board feet

2-by-4 = 5 ⅓ board feet

2-by-6 = 8 board feet

8'

will help you buy what you need at a reasonable cost.

• **Species:** Ask for a specific wood species, rather than a broad family name. For example, order hard maple, not simply maple. To be sure you get what you want, learn the botanical name of the wood you want and ask for it.

• **Quantity:** When ordering wood, specify whether you want the stock in board feet or lineal feet. A lineal foot is merely an expression of a board's length, regardless of its width or thickness. The board foot is a specific volume of wood; it is usually necessary for ordering hardwoods, which are often available in random widths only. See page 16 for information about calculating board feet.

• **Size:** Wood is also sold in nominal rather than finished sizes, so you need to make allowances for the difference when ordering surfaced lumber. A 2-by-4 is actually 1½ inches-by-3½ inches. The thickness of hardwoods is often expressed as a fraction in quarters of an inch. A 1½-inch-thick hardwood board, for example, is often expressed as 6/4. The nominal and real dimensions of unsurfaced, green boards are the same.

• **Surfacing:** Surfacing refers to how the stock is prepared at the mill before it comes to the lumberyard. Softwood lumber is usually surfaced on both faces; hardwood is often sold rough. If you have a planer and jointer, buying rough lumber and surfacing it yourself will prove less expensive.

• **Seasoning:** Lumber is sold either kiln dried (KD), air dried (AD), or green. Kiln-dried wood is generally the most stable. It has a moisture content (MC) of 8 percent, whereas air-dried lumber has a MC of 12 to 20 percent.

• **Grade:** Within the higher hardwood grades, the primary difference between the various grades is appearance rather than strength. Considering the difference in price, it is best to reserve the best stock for the visible parts of your projects, using less expensive, lower-grade wood for hidden components. Consult you lumber dealer for a chart of the different grades available.

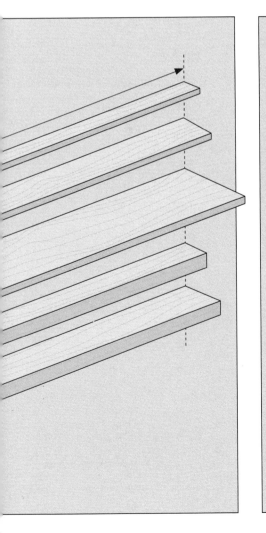

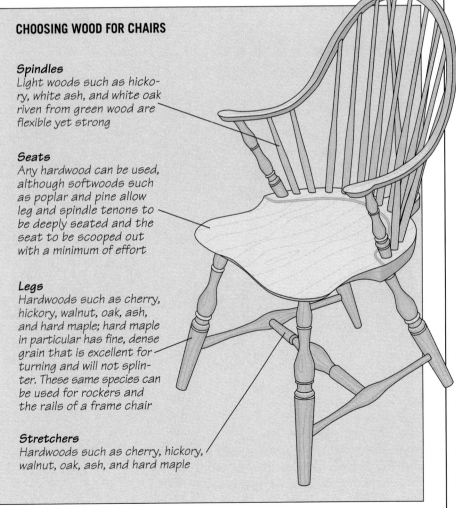

CHOOSING WOOD FOR CHAIRS

Spindles
Light woods such as hickory, white ash, and white oak riven from green wood are flexible yet strong

Seats
Any hardwood can be used, although softwoods such as poplar and pine allow leg and spindle tenons to be deeply seated and the seat to be scooped out with a minimum of effort

Legs
Hardwoods such as cherry, hickory, walnut, oak, ash, and hard maple; hard maple in particular has fine, dense grain that is excellent for turning and will not splinter. These same species can be used for rockers and the rails of a frame chair

Stretchers
Hardwoods such as cherry, hickory, walnut, oak, ash, and hard maple

A GALLERY OF CHAIR STYLES

Apart from the common thread of providing seating and a set of legs to support the seat, chairs can be as different as the craftsmen who build them and the people for whom they are made. The history of chair design is one of individual innovation blended with the technology and tastes prevailing in the chair maker's lifetime.

The remaining pages of this chapter present a sampling of some of the more influential designs of the past 2500 years. Some of these styles are named after the furniture maker who developed them, like Thomas Chippendale or Sam Maloof. Others are associated with the monarch in power when the style flourished, such as Queen Anne. Still others represent a specific design movement, like Mission or Art Nouveau.

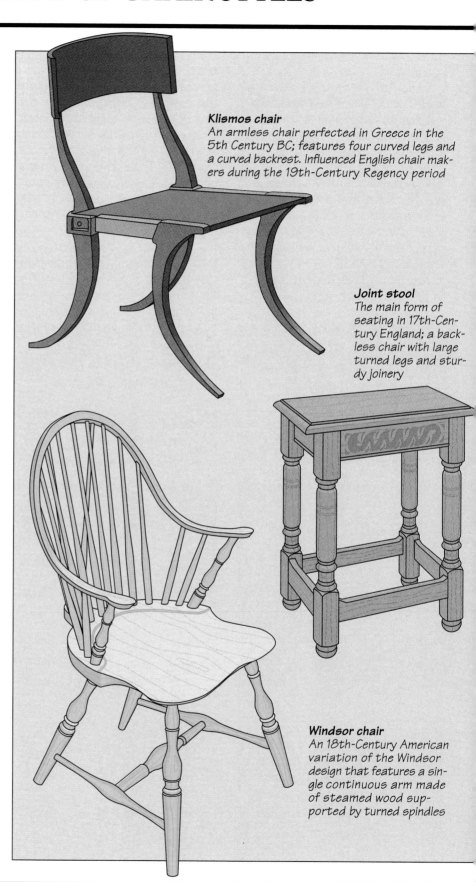

Klismos chair
An armless chair perfected in Greece in the 5th Century BC; features four curved legs and a curved backrest. Influenced English chair makers during the 19th-Century Regency period

Joint stool
The main form of seating in 17th-Century England; a backless chair with large turned legs and sturdy joinery

Windsor chair
An 18th-Century American variation of the Windsor design that features a single continuous arm made of steamed wood supported by turned spindles

Toronto furniture maker Michael Fortune contrasts the warmth of exotic hardwood with modern design in his chairs. The Macassar ebony armchair shown above features laminated curved arms and legs, and fine details such as wool and silver thread upholstery and silver wire inlay set into the slats.

Queen Anne chair
An early 18th-Century British design marked by high backrests and gentle, flowing lines. The cabriole legs give the chair a graceful balance and the backrest is curved to provide comfort; such chairs were often decorated with Oriental motifs as in the example shown

Chippendale chair
Features cabriole legs with claw-and-ball feet, carved shell motifs, and a carved-rail backrest; the example shown was built in Philadelphia in the late 18th-Century in the American Chippendale style

Shaker rocker
A functional and elegant ladder-back rocking chair; the simple finials at the tops of the legs and the woven seat are typical of the spare, economical Shaker style of mid-19th-Century America

Regency chair
Characterized by turned legs, lion's-paw arm supports, pictorial panels, and cane seat covered with a cushion. Dates from the early 19th-Century.

American Sheraton side chair
An early 19th-Century side chair in the American Regency style; the reeding and brass paw feet are hallmarks of the designer, New York chair maker Duncan Phyfe

Ladder-back chair
An enduring country chair design popularized by the Shakers and typically made from green wood; the posts and rungs are riven and the rear legs are steam-bent

Vienna chair
A late 19th-Century chair designed by Frenchman Michael Thonet; its solid wood parts were bent into curved shapes, a development that revolutionized chair making

Mission armchair
Early 20th-Century American offshoot of the Arts-and-Crafts school of design. Made from stained oak with closely spaced spindles, this armchair represents a return to plain, unadorned handcrafting

Frank Lloyd Wright spindle chair
An undecorated and austere side chair with a very high back rest and linear design; its straight-edged parts were designed for mass production

Art Nouveau chair
A high-backed chair designed in 1900 by architect and painter Charles Rennie Mackintosh that contrasts straight lines and geometric forms with gentle curves

Adirondack chair
A popular American outdoor chair from the early 1900s; typically made from pine and assembled with wooden pegs

Rietveld chair
Dutch designer Gerrit Thomas Rietveld's 1918 chair features striking colors and modular elements assembled without joinery; its straight lines forming complex geometric patterns represent a radical departure from traditional chair design

Maloof rocker
A rocking chair with laminated rockers designed by American furniture maker Sam Maloof; its sculptural and organic design typifies the Handicraft Revival of the 1970s

FRAME CHAIRS

Because they are curved to fit the shape of the human back, the back and crest rails of a frame chair can make boring mortises for the slats difficult. The shop-made jig shown above features a curved table to hold the rails squarely as the mortises are routed.

The frame chair is as simple and as sturdy as its workaday name implies. Its basic but elegant design has changed little over hundreds of years. This longevity of style owes much to its clean lines, but also to a robust structure marked by a frame that distributes weight and stress equally around to all the joints.

The principal joinery used in making frame chairs is the stalwart mortise-and-tenon, noted for its ability to withstand tension, shear, racking, and other types of stress that chairs must endure. Blind mortise-and-tenons are used to connect front and back rails to the legs; angled tenons attach the side rails; and rounded slats fit into round mortises in the crest and back rails. Corner blocks fastened to the seat rails help keep the joinery solid and tight over a lifetime of use.

Designing a frame chair carefully is as important as assembling it. Start with a design that will suit the anatomy of the chair's eventual user *(page 14)*; and plan the dimensions of the parts so the chair will fit into its surroundings. Before you buy your stock, draw full-sized templates of the seat *(page 26)*, the rear legs *(page 28)*, and the back rails *(page 32)*. Not only will these templates help you develop a cutting list; they will also enable you to determine the precise sizes of the parts, and show you how to join them.

The frame chair structure allows considerable freedom of design. For example, arms can be incorporated to add comfort or esthetic effect *(page 110)*, stretchers can be installed between the legs, and there are a number of different seats you can install. See the chapter on seats *(page 70)* for a gallery of designs. Even the smaller details can be varied: The front legs can be turned, the curve of the back legs and slats can be given a unique bend, and decorative beads can be milled in the rails. The crest rail can also be given a different shape than the one shown in this chapter or be embellished with stenciling or marquetry.

The basic design of a frame chair can be embellished with decorative details such as turned front legs, beading around the seat rails, rounded slats, and curved crest rails. The sculpted seat is screwed to the seat rails.

ANATOMY OF A FRAME CHAIR

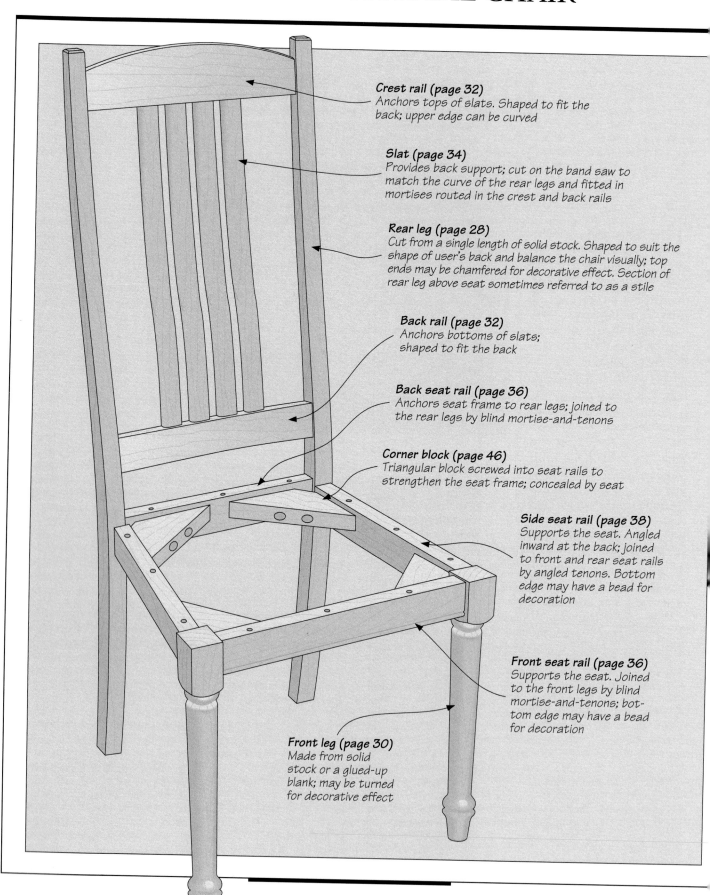

Crest rail (page 32)
Anchors tops of slats. Shaped to fit the back; upper edge can be curved

Slat (page 34)
Provides back support; cut on the band saw to match the curve of the rear legs and fitted in mortises routed in the crest and back rails

Rear leg (page 28)
Cut from a single length of solid stock. Shaped to suit the shape of user's back and balance the chair visually; top ends may be chamfered for decorative effect. Section of rear leg above seat sometimes referred to as a stile

Back rail (page 32)
Anchors bottoms of slats; shaped to fit the back

Back seat rail (page 36)
Anchors seat frame to rear legs; joined to the rear legs by blind mortise-and-tenons

Corner block (page 46)
Triangular block screwed into seat rails to strengthen the seat frame; concealed by seat

Side seat rail (page 38)
Supports the seat. Angled inward at the back; joined to front and rear seat rails by angled tenons. Bottom edge may have a bead for decoration

Front seat rail (page 36)
Supports the seat. Joined to the front legs by blind mortise-and-tenons; bottom edge may have a bead for decoration

Front leg (page 30)
Made from solid stock or a glued-up blank; may be turned for decorative effect

ANGLED TENON-AND-MORTISE

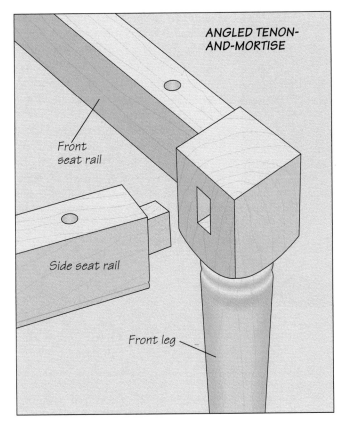

Front seat rail

Side seat rail

Front leg

BLIND MORTISE-AND-TENON

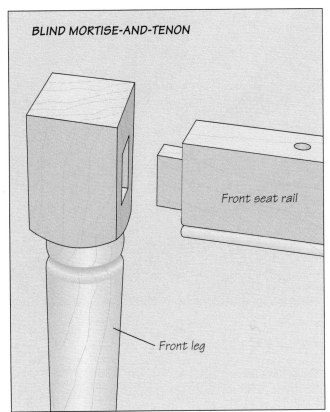

Front seat rail

Front leg

ROUNDED MORTISE-AND-TENON

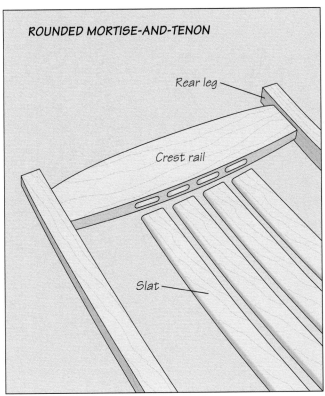

Rear leg

Crest rail

Slat

CORNER BLOCK

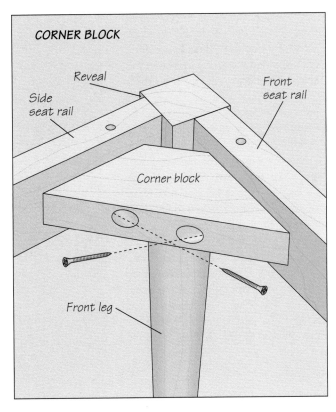

Reveal

Side seat rail

Front seat rail

Corner block

Front leg

DESIGNING THE CHAIR

Shop-made templates for frame chairs are like wooden blueprints drawn to scale, providing the exact dimensions of all the frame pieces as well as the positions of their mortises and tenons. Four main templates are typically required for a chair: one for the legs and rails, shown below—called the seat template—one for the rear legs (page 28), and two for the back rails (page 32). After the templates are drawn, they are cut to shape on the band saw. The leg template shown at left will be used to shape the rear legs. Finished templates can be set aside and kept for future projects.

MAKING THE SEAT TEMPLATE

1 Outlining the legs and rails

Mark out the seat template on a piece of plywood or hardboard. Start by drawing a rectangle to frame the seat, making its length equal to the width of the chair at the front—typically 18 inches. The rectangle's width is equal to the chair's depth, which should be slightly less than the chair width; in this case, the chair depth is 17½ inches. As shown at right, a frame chair seat is usually trapezoidal; make the back narrower than its front; in this example, 15 inches. In the front corners of the rectangle, draw in the two front legs, 1¾ inches square. Then draw in the rear legs, making them wide enough to accommodate the tenons in the back and side rails; stock that is 1 inch thick by 2 inches wide should be sufficient. Next, connect the legs with reveal lines offset ¼ inch from the outside edges of the legs. The lines represent the outside faces of the rails. The offset makes the chair more visually appealing than if the parts were flush. Draw in the inside faces of the rails so the pieces will be 1 inch thick.

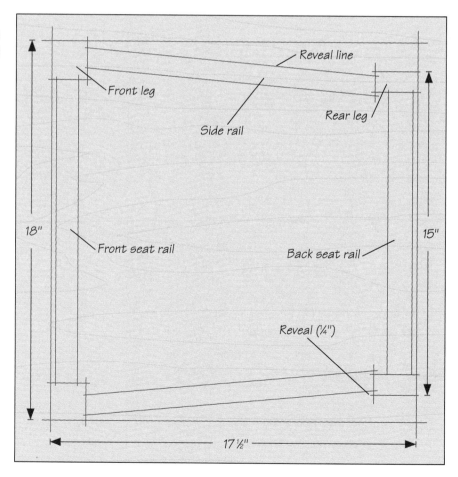

Reveal line

Front leg

Rear leg

Side rail

18"

15"

Front seat rail

Back seat rail

Reveal (¼")

17½"

2 Outlining the tenons

Due to the trapezoidal form of the chair seat, the tenons joining the side rails to the legs must be angled. Start by drawing in the tenons between the side rails and the rear legs. Mark the center of the contact area between one of the side rails and rear leg. Then, assuming ⅜-inch-thick tenons, mark the tenon cheeks, locating each one ³⁄₁₆ inch from your center mark. As shown at right, make the tenon cheeks parallel to the faces of the leg; this will allow you to rout straight mortises in the legs. Make the tenon ¾ inch long. Repeat to draw in the angled tenon at the end of the other side rail. Mark the angled tenons joining the side rails to the front legs so they will be the mirror-image of those at the back end. If, for example, a tenon cheek is ¼ inch from the outside face of the rail at its back end, it should be ¼ inch from the inside face of the rail at the front. Next, draw in standard blind tenons joining the front and back rails to the legs. The tenons in the back rail should be centered in the rail, whereas those in the front rail must be offset toward the rail's outside face to avoid contacting the angled tenons in the side rails. Make sure that there is at least ¼ of space between the tenons in the front legs.

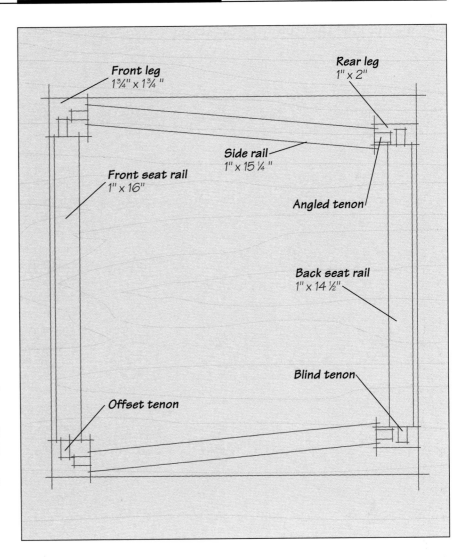

Front leg
1¾" x 1¾"

Rear leg
1" x 2"

Side rail
1" x 15¼"

Angled tenon

Front seat rail
1" x 16"

Back seat rail
1" x 14½"

Blind tenon

Offset tenon

FRAME CHAIR CUTTING LIST

PART	QUANTITY	DIMENSIONS
Front legs	2	1¾" x 1¾" x 16½"
Rear legs	2	1" x 6" x 42"
Front seat rail	1	1" x 2" x 16"
Back seat rail	1	1" x 2" x 14½"
Side rails	2	1" x 2" x 15¼"
Crest rails	1	1⅜" x 3½" x 14½"
Back rail	1	1⅜" x 2" x 14½"
Slats	4	⅜" x 1¼" x 18½"

Making a cutting list

Once you have completed the seat template, you can begin compiling your cutting list for the chair *(left)*. As shown, the cutting list should list the individual chair parts, how many of each is needed, and the dimensions of each part. Since the template is drawn to scale, you can take the measurements of the rails directly from it. The crest and back rails *(page 24)* will be the same length as the back seat rail and a little thicker. The crest rail is also wider than the other rails. You will not be able to determine the precise size of the slats and the length of the legs until the leg templates are done *(page 28)*. Refer to page 16 for information on using a cutting list to determine how much lumber you need to buy.

MAKING THE TEMPLATE FOR THE REAR LEGS

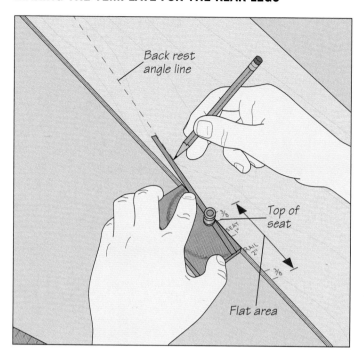

Back rest angle line

Top of seat

Flat area

1 Marking the angle of the back rest
Cut a piece of plywood or hardboard to the length of the rear legs—in this case, about 42 inches. Start by marking the locations of the seat and side rails on one edge of the template. The top of the seat should typically be about 17½ inches from the bottom of the leg. Make the seat 1 inch thick and mark the 2-inch-wide rail directly below it. These marks define a flat section along the leg where the rails and seat will be joined to the leg. Extend the length of the flat section by ⅜ inch above and below it. This will help you avoid curving the flat section—and creating imprecise joinery—when you later sand the leg *(page 31)*. Then use a protractor and a pencil to draw a line for the angle of the back rest above the flat section *(left)*; a 10° angle will yield a chair back that most people find comfortable, but any angle between 0° and 20° is acceptable. Extend the line with a carpenter's square to the top of the template (as represented by the dotted line in the illustration).

2 Drawing the curve of the back rest
To convert the angled line you marked in step 1 into a natural curve, cut a thin strip of springy wood roughly one-half the template's length. Using clamps and a stop block, secure the strip on edge on the template so that one face is flush with the top of your line. Then, holding the strip near its other end, gently bend it toward the line until it is flush with the front edge of the template at the flat area. Keeping the strip firmly in place, run a pencil along it to define the curve of the legs above the seat *(right)*.

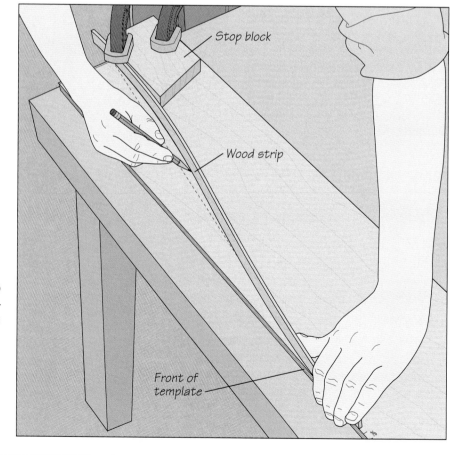

Stop block

Wood strip

Front of template

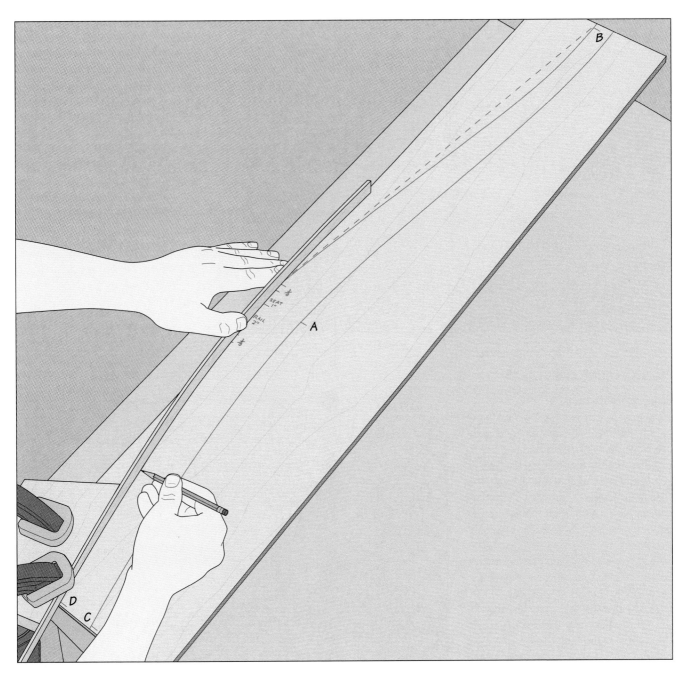

3 Completing the rear-leg template

Complete the top half of the template by drawing a curve roughly parallel to the one you made in step 2. To define the beginning and end of the curve, mark a point directly opposite the rail mark 2 inches from the front edge of the template (mark A in the illustration above). Since the leg tapers toward the top, mark a point at the top that is only 1 inch from the first curve (mark B). Join the two marks using the same method shown in step 2. For the bottom of the leg, start with the curve at the back. Mark a point at the bottom (mark C) that is 1 inch closer to the front edge of the template than mark B; this ensures that the back of the leg at the bottom will not extend beyond the top and trip up someone passing the chair from behind. Join points A and C. Finish the template by drawing the curve for the front of the leg at the bottom. For balance, esthetics, and strength, mark a point at the bottom (mark D) so the leg's width at the floor will be midway between its width at the rail and the top, or 1½ inches. Use a pencil and the springy wood strip to draw the curve (above).

MAKING THE LEGS

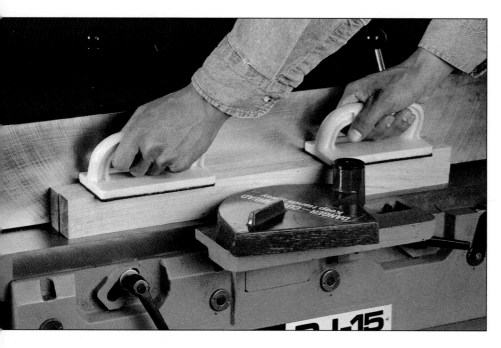

A blank for one of the front legs of a frame chair is trued on a jointer. Push blocks are used to safeguard the operator's hands from the cutterhead knives. The stock for chair legs should be free of defects like knots, checks, and splits.

MAKING FRONT LEG BLANKS

Gluing up the leg blanks

If the front legs of your chair will be thicker than the stock you have on hand, you can make leg blanks by face-gluing boards together. Cut the stock so the blanks will be slightly larger than the final size of the legs. In this case, the legs will be 1¾ inches square; their length, from the floor to the bottom of the seat, is typically 17½ inches. Glue up both blanks in a single setup. Spread glue on the mating surfaces of the boards, then use as many bar clamps as necessary to support the stock at 4-inch intervals, alternating the clamps between the top and bottom of the stock. Tighten the clamps *(right)* until there are no gaps between the boards and a thin bead of glue squeezes out of the joints. After the adhesive has cured, joint an edge and face of each blank, plane or rip them to their final width and thickness, and crosscut them to length.

MAKING THE REAR LEGS

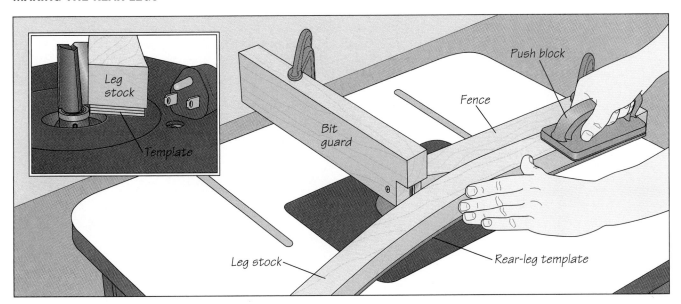

1 Shaping the legs

Use the rear-leg template *(page 29)* to outline the patterns on two pieces of stock planed to a thickness of 1 inch. Cut away most of the waste with a saber saw or band saw, leaving about ¹⁄₁₆ inch of wood beyond the cutting lines. Attach the template to one of the leg pieces using strong double-sided tape, then finish shaping the legs on a router table. Install a piloted straight bit in the router, mount the tool in a table, and set the depth of cut so that the pilot bearing will rub only on the template *(inset)*. Fashion a guard for the bit and a fence for the template and stock to ride against on the infeed side of the table. Screw the guard and fence together and clamp them to the table. Press the template against the pilot bearing as you feed the stock across the table; use a push block to finish the cut *(above)*. Turn the stock around to shape the other side of the leg. Then tape the template to the other leg piece and repeat the operation to shape it.

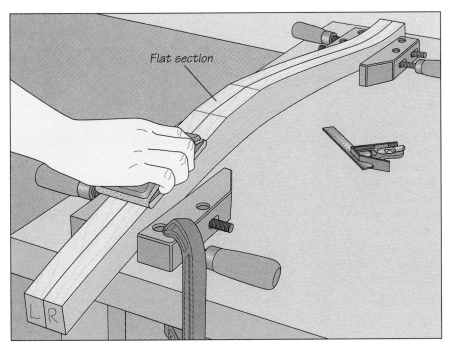

2 Smoothing the legs

Once the legs have been shaped, label one as the right leg and the other as the left on their bottom ends. Then use handscrews to clamp the legs face to face, edges flush, and secure the handscrews to a work surface so the front edges of the legs are facing up. Referring to the template, use a pencil and a combination square to mark the flat section on the legs' edges. Then use a sanding block to smooth the edges of the rails, being careful to avoid the flat area. Use progressively finer-grit sandpaper until the surface is smooth. Sand the back edges of the legs the same way.

MAKING THE BACKREST

MAKING THE BACK-RAIL AND CREST-RAIL TEMPLATES

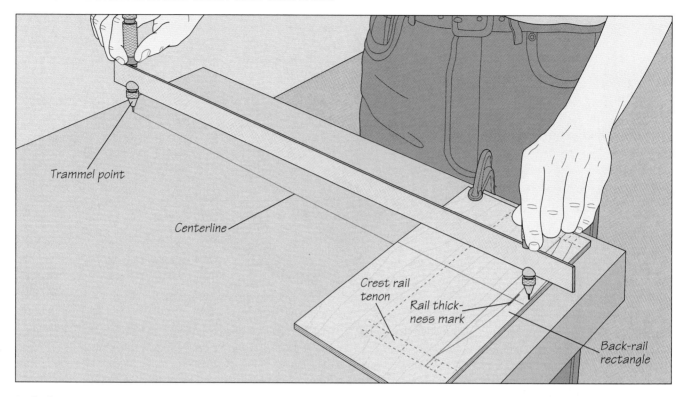

Designing the templates

Since the back and crest rails of the frame chair share the same curvature, make templates for both pieces on a single piece of plywood or hardboard clamped to a work surface. Start with the back-rail template, drawing a rectangle as long as the gap between the rear legs and as wide as the rail stock thickness—about 1½ to 2 inches. Then mark a line down the center of the rectangle, extending it across the template and your work surface. Mark the thickness of the back rail on the centerline, in this case 1 inch from the top of the rectangle. Next, use trammel points to draw an arc on the template that intersects your rail thickness mark and the bottom corners of the rectangle. Draw a second arc parallel to the first, outlining the back rail *(above)*. You will use this outline to cut both the back and crest rails to thickness *(page 36)*. Then draw a third arc outlining the top of the crest rail *(right)*. Complete the templates by drawing in the sides and bottom edge of the crest rail outline, and the tenons for both rails. (These elements are represented by dotted lines in the illustrations.) Cut out the templates and trace their outlines on your rail blanks. Trace the back rail outline on the top edges of both the back and crest rail blanks. Trace the crest rail outline on the face of your crest rail blank. Finally, saw blind tenons at the ends of both rails *(page 36)*, then cut the rails on the band saw *(page 33)*.

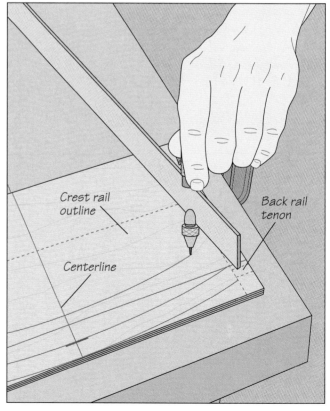

CUTTING THE CREST RAIL

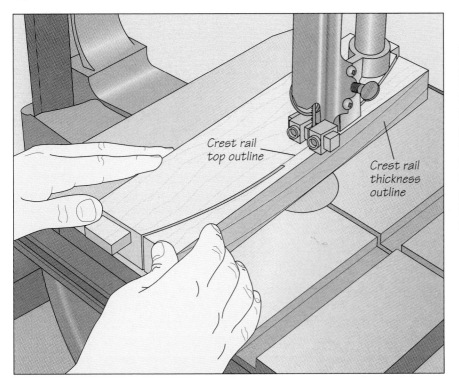

Crest rail top outline

Crest rail thickness outline

1 Cutting the top edge of the rail
Set the crest rail blank face-up on the band saw table, aligning the blade just to the waste side of the cutting line for the top of the rail. Feed the stock into the blade, turn off the saw about halfway through the cut, and remove the workpiece. Then cut along the same line from the opposite end. To avoid detaching the waste piece from the blank and losing the marked outline on the top edge of the rail, stop the cut about ¼ inch from the first kerf, leaving a short bridge between the two cuts *(left)*.

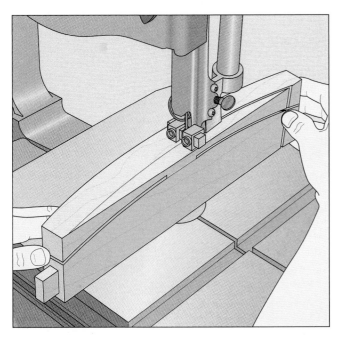

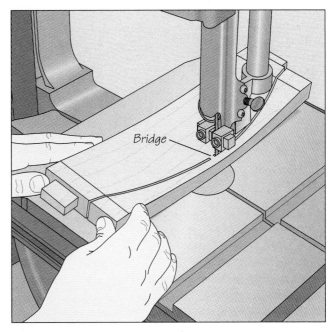

Bridge

2 Sawing the crest rail to thickness
Turn the rail blank so the marked outline on its top edge is facing up. Cut along both marked lines *(above)*. This time, complete the cut, letting the waste fall away. (This same cut is used to saw the back rail to thickness.)

3 Severing the bridge
Rotate the crest rail blank so the first face you cut is facing up. With the saw turned off, feed the blade into the kerf. Then turn on the saw and cut through the bridge to release the waste piece *(above)*.

MAKING THE SLATS

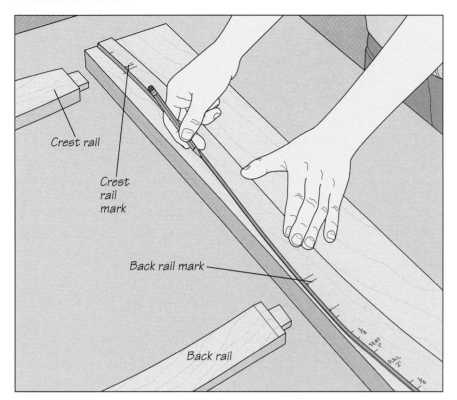

Crest rail

Crest rail mark

Back rail mark

Back rail

1 Determining the curve of the slats
Cut a blank wide enough to yield the number of slats you need for the chair. The thickness of the blank will determine the width of the slats, so make it 1 to 2 inches thick. Plan on producing an even number of slats so there will not be a single slat in the middle of the back rest exerting pressure on the chair user's spine. Use the rear-leg template *(page 29)* to mark the curve of the slats. Mark the locations of the crest and back rails on the template, and add marks ½ inch beyond the first two to represent the ends of the slats that will fit into mortises in the rails. Next, place the template on the blank so the top ends are flush and mark the curve of the template on the blank with a pencil *(left)*. Then cut along your marked line on the band saw and smooth the cut edge *(step 4)*.

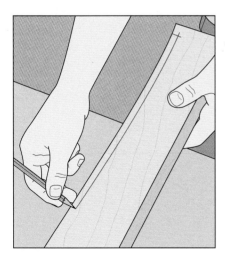

2 Outlining the first slat
Transfer the slat end marks from the template to the blank. Then, with a pencil held between your thumb and index finger, run your middle finger along the curved edge of the blank to mark a cutting line parallel to the edge and ⅜ inch from it *(above)*. You can also use a marking gauge to scribe the cutting line.

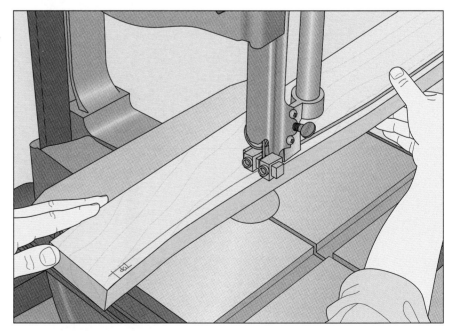

3 Cutting the first slat
Label the top and bottom ends of the slat, then cut the slat on the band saw *(above)*, keeping your hands well clear of the blade. Repeat steps 2 and 3 to produce the number of slats you need.

4 Smoothing the slats

Sand the slats by hand or with a spindle sander *(right)*, using progressively finer-grit sandpaper sleeves until the slats are smooth. With your right hand, feed the slats against the direction of the sanding drum's rotation while applying pressure with your left hand.

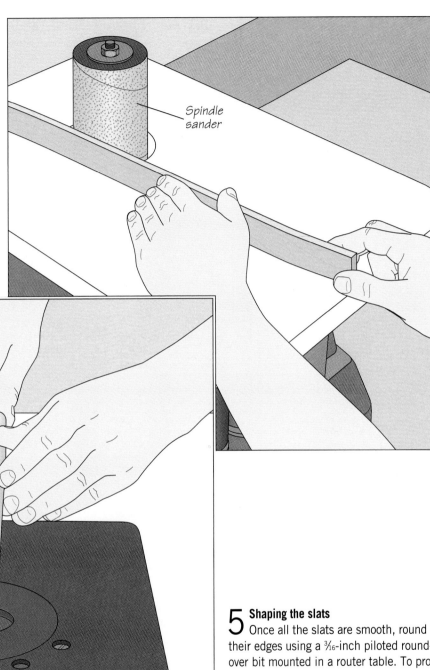

Spindle sander

5 Shaping the slats

Once all the slats are smooth, round their edges using a ³⁄₁₆-inch piloted round-over bit mounted in a router table. To provide a bearing surface for the slats, install the same fence and bit guard you used to shape the rear legs *(page 31)*. Set the height and depth of cut using a piece of stock the same thickness as your slats. Then round the edges of each slat, feeding them into the bit with your right hand while applying pressure against the fence with your left *(left)*. Keep your hands well clear of the bit throughout the operation.

A bench-mounted mortiser cuts a mortise in the front leg of a chair, readying the leg for a rail tenon. The model shown above can produce perfectly square mortises up to 3 inches deep. Because it excels at resisting racking and other stresses that chairs must undergo, the mortise-and-tenon is the joint of choice for connecting frame chair parts. Use standard blind tenons to join the front and back seat rails as well as the crest and back rails to the legs (right); cut angled blind tenons (page 38) to fix the side seat rails to the legs.

CUTTING STANDARD BLIND TENONS

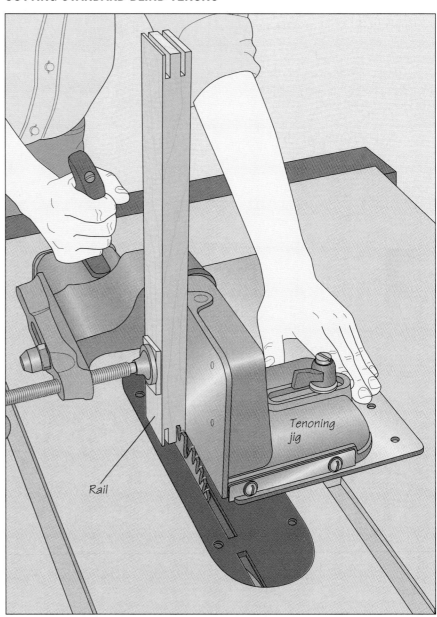

Tenoning jig

Rail

1 Sawing the tenon cheeks

You can cut standard blind tenons in the rails quickly and accurately on your table saw with a commercial tenoning jig. The model above slides in the miter slot. Outline the tenons on the ends of the rails, using your seat template *(page 27)* as a guide. Set the cutting height to the tenon length. Using a wood pad to protect the workpiece, clamp a rail to the jig end-up. Adjust the jig sideways to align one of the tenon marks with the blade. After making the first cut, turn the rail around to cut the other tenon cheek. If you are cutting an offset tenon like the one shown, in which the tenon is not centered on the end of the rail, you will have to reposition the jig to saw the second cheek. Repeat the cuts at the other end of the rail *(above)* and at both ends of the remaining rails.

2 Sawing the tenon shoulders

Screw a board to the miter gauge as an extension. Then, holding a rail against the extension, adjust the cutting height to the depth of the tenon shoulder. Align the shoulder with the blade, butt a stop block against the workpiece and clamp the block to the extension. Holding the rail against the stop block and the extension, feed the stock with the miter gauge to cut the first shoulder. To saw the opposite shoulder, turn the rail over *(right)*, adjusting the blade height for an offset tenon. To cut the shoulders on the edges of the tenon, make a series of passes with the board on edge until the waste is removed. Repeat to cut the tenons at the other end of the rail and in the remaining rails.

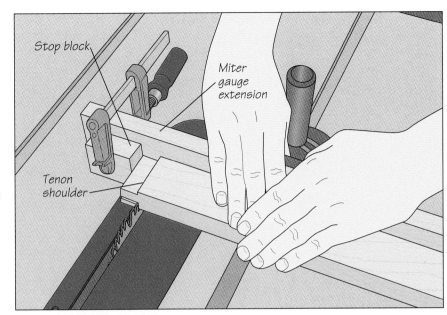

BUILD IT YOURSELF

A TENONING JIG

The shop-made tenoning jig shown below offers a simple and inexpensive way to saw the tenon cheeks in the rails of your chair. Refer to the dimensions suggested in the illustration, making sure the thickness of the spacer and width of the brace allow the jig to slide smoothly along your rip fence without wobbling. Cut the body and brace from ¾-inch plywood and the guide and spacer from solid wood. Saw an oval hole for a handle in one corner of the jig body and attach the guide to the body directly in front of the handle hole, ensuring that the guide is vertical. Screw a small wood block to the body below the handle and attach a toggle clamp to the block. Finally, fasten the spacer and brace in place. To use the jig, place it astride the fence. Butt the workpiece against the jig guide and clamp it in place. Position the fence to align the cutting lines on the workpiece with the blade and slide the jig along the fence to make the cut.

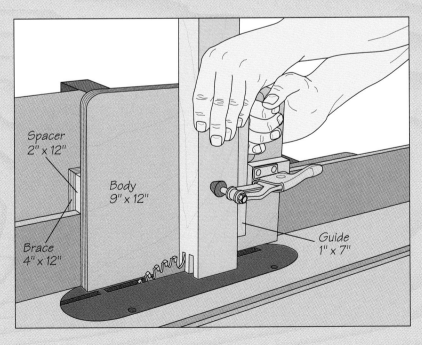

CUTTING ANGLED TENONS IN THE SIDE RAILS

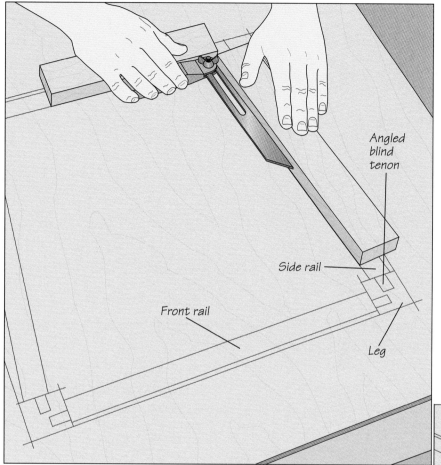

Angled blind tenon

Side rail

Front rail

Leg

1 **Setting the table saw blade angle**
Once you have cut the tenons in the front and back seat rails and the back and crest rails, cut the blind angled tenons in the side rails. To set the blade angle on your table saw for cutting the angled tenon cheeks, use the seat template *(page 27)* as a guide. Align two boards along a back corner of the template and adjust a sliding bevel to the angle formed by the boards *(left)*.

2 **Adjusting the cutting width and height**
Install a dado head on your saw and transfer the angle from the sliding bevel to the blades. Install an auxiliary wooden fence on the rip fence and notch it with the dado head. Then set a cutting width of ¾ inch and a height of ⅛ inch. Feed a scrap piece the same size as your stock face down into the dado head to make test cuts across both ends, as shown in step 3. Then position the test piece on the seat template directly over one of the side rails *(right)*. The shoulder lines on the piece and the template should line up; if not, increase the cutting width and make another sets of cuts, continuing until the shoulders align. Adjust the cutting height until the tenon cheeks on the piece line up with the template.

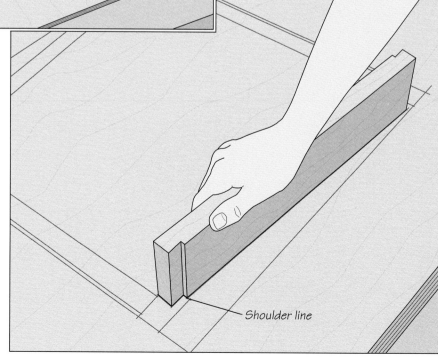

Shoulder line

Shoulder line

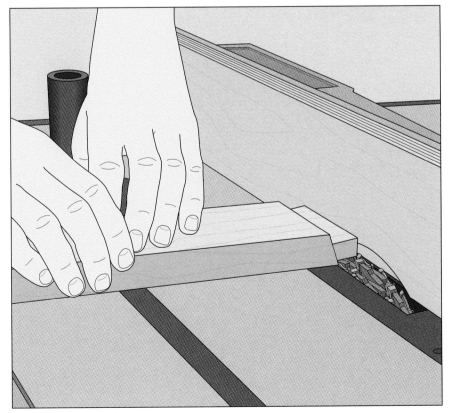

3 Cutting the tenon cheeks

Once the cutting width and height of the dado head have been properly set, put the test piece aside and make the cuts on the side rails. Use the miter gauge and fence to guide the board for one pass, then turn the board over and repeat the cut at the other end *(above)*. Cut the corresponding cheeks in the other side rail. To set up the saw for the other side of the cheeks, set one of the rails on edge and use the sliding bevel to extend the shoulder line across the edge of the board *(inset)*. Then move the rip fence to the other side of the dado head, and reposition and notch the auxiliary fence accordingly. Align the shoulder mark with the outside blade of the dado head and butt the fence against the end of the stock. Leaving the angle of the dado head unchanged, cut the remaining cheeks *(left)* in both rails the same way you cut the first set. (Make these cuts on the test piece first, and then adjust the cutting width and height, as necessary.)

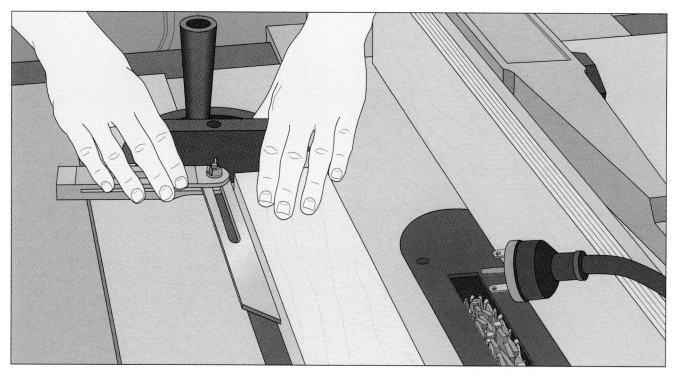

4 Setting up the saw for the tenon shoulders
Adjust the angle of the dado head to 90°. Holding a board parallel to the miter slot, use the sliding bevel to set the miter gauge to the same angle used to adjust the blades in step 1 *(above)*. Butt one of the side rails on edge against the miter gauge. The shoulder should be parallel to the rip fence; if not, turn the rail over onto its other edge. Set the width of cut to the width of the cheek and adjust the dado head to the desired cutting height.

5 Cutting the tenon shoulders
Like the tenon cheeks, the shoulders are cut in two steps. For the first set of cuts, guide the workpiece on edge using the miter gauge and fence *(right)*, then turn the board around and repeat the cut at the other end of the same edge. Saw the corresponding shoulders on the other rail. To make the second set of cuts, use the sliding bevel as in step 4 to angle the miter gauge in the opposite direction. Cut the remaining shoulders on the other edges of both rails the same way you made the first two.

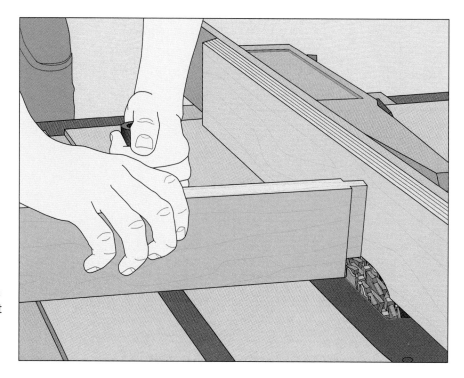

MORTISING THE LEGS FOR THE SEAT RAILS

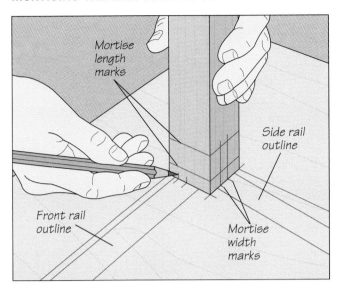

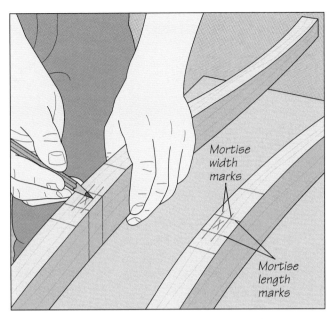

1 Marking mortises in the front legs

Mark the length of the seat rail mortises on the front legs, using a tenon on the front rail as a guide. To mark the width of the mortises, position a leg on the seat template. Since you are marking on the top of the template, place the right leg in the left-hand corner of the template and the left leg in the right-hand corner. Extend the tenon marks on the template onto the leg to outline the width of the mortises for the front and side rail tenons *(above)*. Then extend the width lines across the length marks. Bore the mortises with a mortiser *(page 36)* or a jig *(page 42)* before turning the legs.

2 Marking the mortises in the rear legs

Use your leg template to mark the location of the side seat rail on each rear leg. Then use the tenon of the side seat rail to outline the length of the mortises on the legs. Extend the lines onto the inside face of each leg. To mark the mortise width, measure the position and thickness of the side rail tenon on the seat template, measure the position of the side rail mortise on each rear leg, and transfer your measurement to the legs *(above)*. Repeat to outline the mortises for the back rail tenons.

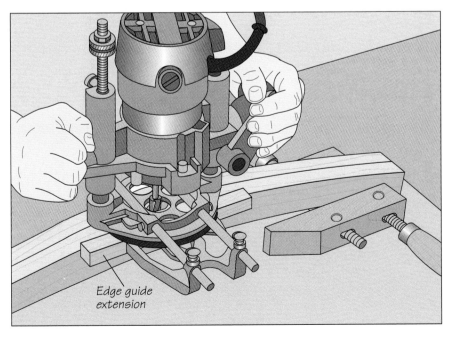

3 Routing the mortises in the rear legs

Secure the legs face to face to a work surface so that two matching mortise outlines are facing up and perfectly aligned. Then install a ⅜-inch mortising bit in a plunge router; also install a commercial edge guide fitted with a wooden extension. Butt the edge guide against the leg (which is not curved at this point), adjust it to center the bit over one of the mortise outlines and rout the mortise with a series of successively deeper passes until it is ⅛ inch deeper than the tenon length. Keep the edge guide flush against the leg throughout the cuts *(left)*. Repeat for the mortise in the other leg and for the adjacent edges of both legs. Square the corners of the mortises with a chisel.

A MORTISING JIG FOR CHAIR LEGS
Paired with a router, the jig shown below can help you mortise chair legs without the use of more specialized tools. Cut the jig top and edge guide from ¾-inch plywood, referring to the illustration for suggested dimensions. Screw the pieces together in an L shape and countersink your fasteners.

To prepare the jig, rout a slot in the top. Cut the slot slightly longer than the mortise outlines in the legs—and wide enough to accept the template guide you will use with the bit.

To use the jig, clamp the leg to the edge guide so that the top is flush against the workpiece and the slot is centered over the mortise outline on the leg; place a shim between the leg and the guide, if necessary. Secure the edge guide in a bench vise and install a ⅜-inch mortising bit and template guide in your router. Align the bit with the end of the mortise outline,

butt a stop block against the router base plate and clamp the block to the jig top. Then, rout the mortise with a series of successively deeper passes until it is ⅛ inch deeper than the tenon length, riding the template guide against the sides of the slot. Stop each pass when the router contacts the stop block (below, right). Square the corners of the mortise with a chisel.

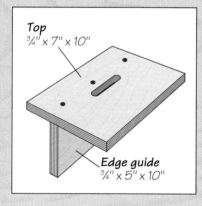

Top
¾" x 7" x 10"

Edge guide
¾" x 5" x 10"

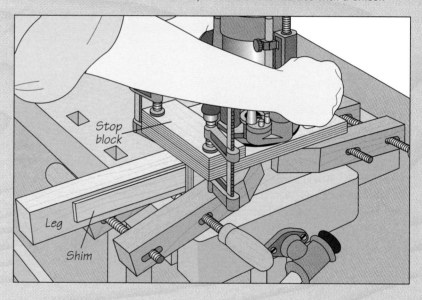

Stop block

Leg

Shim

MORTISING THE REAR LEGS FOR THE BACK AND CREST RAILS

1 Outlining the mortises
Use the tenons on the back and crest rails to mark their mortises on the rear-leg template. Position the template on one of the rear legs and transfer the rail and mortise marks to the workpiece (right). Then transfer the marks from the leg to the other rear leg, butting the two legs together and using a combination square to extend the lines.

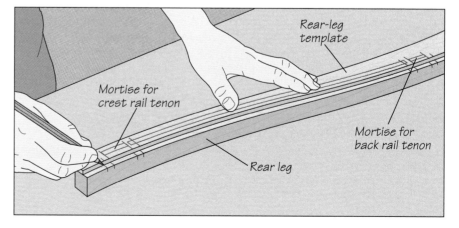

Rear-leg template

Mortise for crest rail tenon

Mortise for back rail tenon

Rear leg

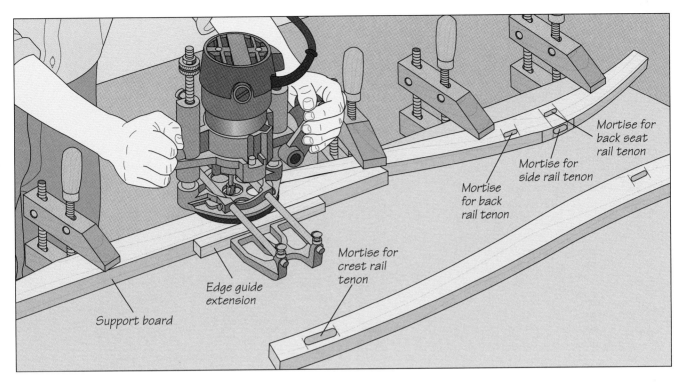

Mortise for
back seat
rail tenon

Mortise for
side rail tenon

Mortise
for back
rail tenon

Mortise for
crest rail
tenon

Edge guide
extension

Support board

2 Routing the mortises

Using a plunge router fitted with an extended edge guide and a ⅜-inch mortising bit, rout the mortises as you did for the seat rail tenons *(page 41)*. To help feed the router in a straight line along the curved section of the rear legs, cut the leg curve into a support board of the same thickness as the legs. Clamp the curved edge of the board to the leg and ride the edge guide along the straight edge of the board as you rout the mortises for the rail tenons *(above)*.

MORTISING THE BACK AND CREST RAILS FOR THE SLATS

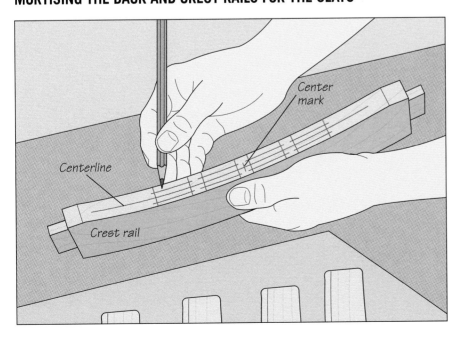

Center
mark

Centerline

Crest rail

Marking the mortises

Mark a centerline along the bottom edge of the crest rail and the top edge of the back rail. Also mark a line across the center of each rail. Working from the center toward the ends, outline the mortises at ½-inch intervals along the centerline *(left)*. Make the mortise length equal to the width of the slats. Once all the mortises are outlined in both rails, rout them *(page 44)*.

A JIG FOR MORTISING CURVED RAILS

The jig shown at right allows you to quickly rout the slat mortises in the curved crest and back rails of a frame chair. Cut all the parts from ¾-inch plywood, except for the curved table, which should be made from solid stock and cut with the same curvature as the rails *(page 33)*; see the illustration for suggested dimensions. Screw the base to the base support so they form an L. Position the base 4 inches from the bottom of the fence and bore two holes through opposite ends of the fence into the base support. Use a router with a straight bit to lengthen the hole on the outfeed side of the fence into a curved slot. Attach the base support to the fence with carriage bolts, washers and wing nuts. Leave the bolt at the infeed end loose enough for the base to pivot when the slotted end is raised or lowered. Next, screw the curved table to the base from underneath.

Remove the sub-base from your router and use it as a template to mark the screw holes and bit clearance hole on the fence. The bottom edge of the clearance hole should line up with the top of the curved table when the table is level.

To use the jig, secure the fence in a vise. Install a ⅜-inch mortising bit in the router, attaching the tool to the jig fence, and adjusting the cutting depth. Set the rail face up on the curved table, butting the top edge against the bit. Loosen the wing nut at the slotted end and adjust the table to center the bit in the middle of one of the mortise outlines, then tighten the nut. Secure the workpiece by clamping hold-downs with curved bottom ends to the fence. Turn on the tool, align the start of the first mortise outline with the bit and push the rail against the fence, plunging the bit into the stock. Withdraw the rail, move it sideways and push it against the fence to rout a hole next to the first. Continue until the entire outline is routed out. Cut the remaining mortises the same way *(above, bottom)*.

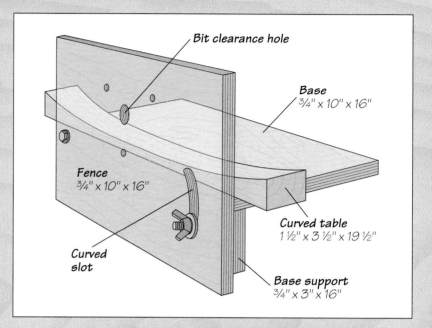

Bit clearance hole

Base
¾" x 10" x 16"

Fence
¾" x 10" x 16"

Curved table
1 ½" x 3 ½" x 19 ½"

Curved slot

Base support
¾" x 3" x 16"

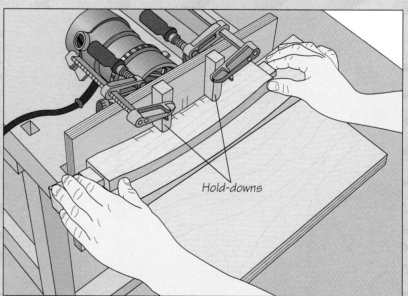

Hold-downs

SMOOTHING THE RAILS, SLATS AND LEGS

1 Sanding the back-rest rails and slats
Before assembling the chair, smooth the surfaces of parts that cannot be sanded after the chair is glued up. Hand-sand parts that would difficult to smooth with a power sander, such as the slats and back-rest rails *(right)*. Use progressively finer-grit sandpaper until the surface is smooth; move to a finer-grit abrasive when the marks left by the coarser sheet are smoothed away.

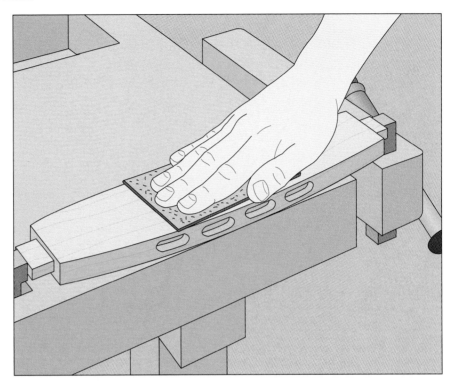

2 Sanding the legs and seat rails
Use a power sander like the belt sander shown below to smooth the remaining chair parts: the seat rails and the legs. Secure your workpiece between bench dogs on a workbench, protecting the stock with wood pads. As with hand-sanding, use progressively finer-grit sanding belts to smooth the stock.

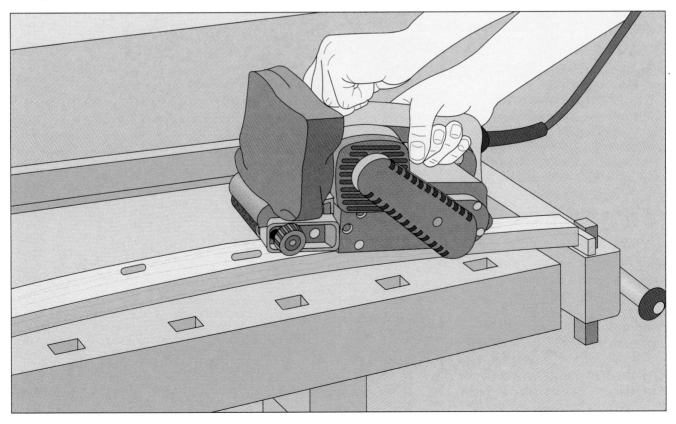

MAKING THE CORNER BLOCKS

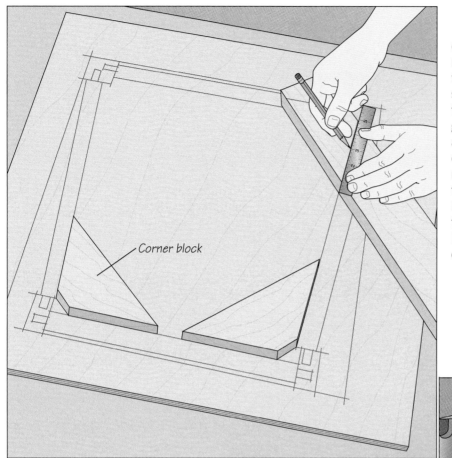

Corner block

Support
board

1 Cutting the blocks
The last step before gluing up the chair is preparing the corner blocks that reinforce the seat frame. Cut the blocks from a board of the same thickness as the seat rails. Start by outlining the blocks on the board, using your seat template as a guide. Place the board on the template across one of the corners so that the grain of the board is diagonal to the grain of the rails. Then extend the lines representing the inside faces of the rails across the board. Cut the block on the band saw, trimming the inside corner to clear the leg. Repeat to mark and cut the remaining corner blocks *(left)*.

2 Preparing the blocks
Bore two screw holes through the corner blocks on your drill press. Starting with a Forstner bit slightly larger than the heads of the screws you will use to install the blocks, hold the block with its long edge facing up and drill shallow pocket holes for recessing the screw heads *(right)*. Clamp a support board to the table to help you keep the block vertical. Once all these holes are drilled, complete the clearance holes through the blocks with a brad-point bit slightly larger than the screw shafts.

ASSEMBLING THE CHAIR

A sharp chisel cuts away dried glue from the joint between the crest rail and rear leg of a chair (right). Squeezed-out adhesive should be removed from all joints; otherwise, the surfaces will be difficult to sand and tend to repel the finish.

GLUING UP THE FRONT AND BACK ASSEMBLIES

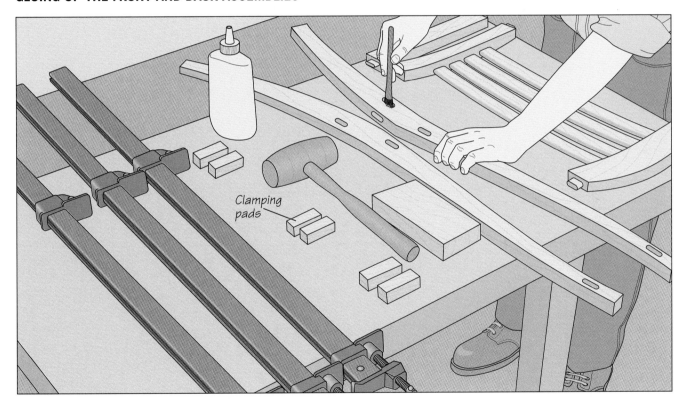

Clamping pads

1 Spreading the glue
A frame chair is assembled in two steps: First, the back and front leg assemblies are glued up separately, as shown above and on page 48, then the leg assemblies are joined with the side seat rails *(page 49)*. Start by test-fitting the chair components—the legs, the crest and back rails, the seat rails, and the slats. Use a chisel to pare away excess wood from any excessively tight joints. If you will be screwing the chair seat to

the seat rails, drill the holes through the rails *(page 77)*. Once the rails are ready, cut a half-dozen wood clamping pads, prepare three bar clamps, then apply glue to the joints of the rear leg assembly. Using a small, stiff-bristled brush, spread adhesive on the rail tenons and in their leg mortises *(above)*. Do not apply any glue on the slats or in their rail mortises; the slats must be free to move.

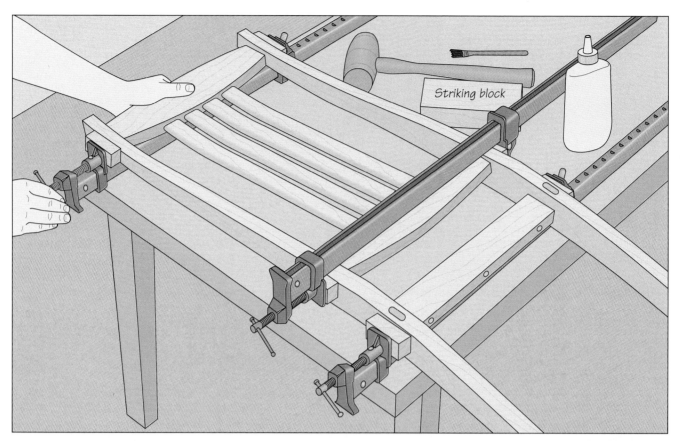

Striking block

2 Gluing up the rear leg assembly

Assemble the back rest, fitting the slats into their mortises in the back and crest rails, then insert the rail tenons into their mortises in one of the rear legs; take care to keep the slats in place. Next, slip the back seat rail into place in the leg, fit the other rear leg onto the rails and tap the assembly together with a wooden mallet; use a striking block to prevent marring the stock. Install the clamps across the three rails, protecting the legs with the pads. Tighten the clamps a little at a time *(above)* until a thin bead of glue squeezes out of the joints.

3 Gluing up the front leg assembly

For the front leg assembly, you will need a single bar clamp and a pair of clamping pads. Glue the front legs to the front seat rail, sighting along the rail to ensure that the legs are perfectly aligned *(right)*. If they are misaligned, slacken the clamp a little, twist the legs into line and retighten. Let the glue in the front and back leg assemblies cure for 24 hours before proceeding to final glue-up.

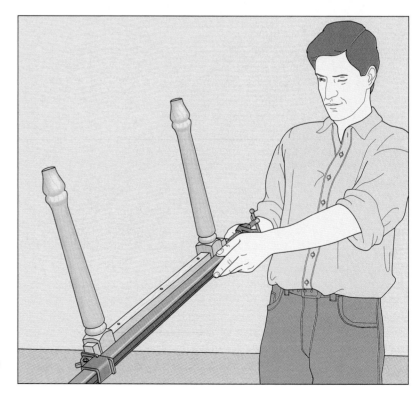

GLUING UP THE CHAIR

1 Gluing the side seat rails to the rear legs
Once the adhesive in the two leg assemblies has cured, remove the clamps and glue the assemblies together with the side seat rails. Assemble the chair on a perfectly flat surface, such as a saw table. Start by clamping a board as long as the front of the chair is wide to the back face of the back seat rail; this clamping board will help you keep the chair square as you assemble it. Set the rear leg assembly on its back, then spread glue on the side rail tenons *(right)* and in their mortises in the legs. Fit the rails into the rear legs.

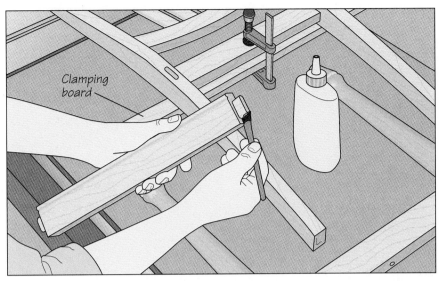

Clamping board

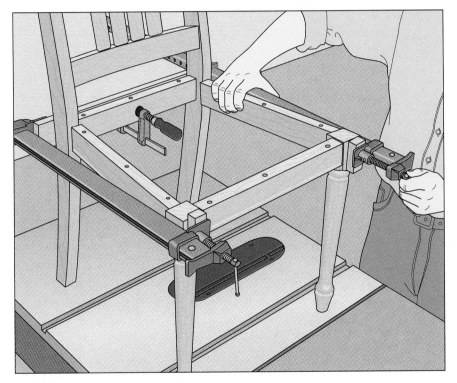

2 Joining the leg assemblies
Working quickly, fit the front leg assembly onto the side seat rails and set the chair upright. Install two clamps along the side rails, protecting the front legs with wood pads. Tighten the clamps *(above)*, then gently rock the chair to ensure that it is level. If not, loosen the clamp on the uneven leg, slide one of its jaws up slightly, and retighten. Check again for level, shifting the clamps as necessary until the chair is level. Also make sure that the top edges of all the seat rails are level with the tops of the front legs; use a mallet and striking block to tap the rails into position, if necessary.

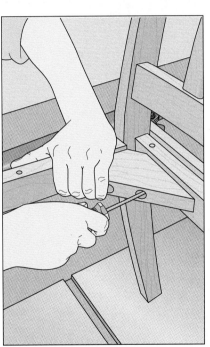

3 Installing the corner blocks
Once the chair is level and the clamps are tightened, spread some glue on the edges of the corner blocks that will contact the seat rails and screw each one in place *(above)*. Drive the screws until there are no gaps between the blocks and the rails and a thin bead of glue squeezes out between the two. Now prepare and install a seat *(page 70)*.

SLAB-AND-STICK CHAIRS

The slats for a ladder-back chair like the one shown on page 50 can be bent dry, using the jig shown above. Made from two thin wood strips face-glued together, each slat is held by a web clamp against a form, which is cut to the desired curve.

The Windsor chair, with its independent back and leg assemblies anchored to a solid seat, and the post-and-rail chair—or simple stick chair— in which the back is an extension of the rear legs, have long been favorites with woodworkers. Windsors are noted for both comfort and elegance, but they are a challenge to build. Most styles call for steam-bending many of the parts, such as the continuous arms. The joints must also be cut to very close tolerances. Simple stick chairs, on the other hand, are easier to assemble; most designs feature simple round mortise-and-tenon joinery.

This chapter will show you how to build a hybrid of these two styles, a slab-and-stick chair like the one shown on page 50. With the solid seat and separate leg-and-back assemblies of the Windsor, this chair can be very comfortable. Like the stick chair, most of its parts are assembled with round mortises and tenons, which simplifies its construction.

Both Windsor and stick chairs are traditionally made of green, or "wet", wood—freshly hewn stock that has not been seasoned or dried. The benefits of working with green wood are many. Wet wood is relatively inexpensive and it is easier to shape and join. Fitting a dry leg tenon into a mortise in a wet chair seat, for example, can make a snug joint even tighter. Once the joint is assembled, the tenon will absorb moisture from the seat, swelling the tenon and shrinking the mortise. Provided that the tolerances are close, such joints may not even require glue.

Although the chair featured in this chapter can be constructed with green wood, the procedures shown in the following pages assume the use of dry, seasoned lumber. As a result, the mortise-and-tenons are glued together. The joints attaching the legs to the seat are reinforced by wedges and the slat-to-back post connections are strengthened by pegs. Although cherry is designated in the cutting list, you can use any wood that can be worked easily and is unlikely to check or crack after the chair is assembled.

As with any piece of furniture, form should follow function. The shape of the seat and the slope of the back shown here represent only one of many design possibilities. The chair you build should conform to the needs of its eventual user. Read the introductory essay by John and Caroline Grew-Sheridan *(page 11)* to learn more about how ergonomics can affect a chair's design.

The chair at left combines a ladder back with a sculpted Windsor-style seat, creating an elegant hybrid that is relatively simple to build. The contrasting wedges in the leg tenons and the concentric rings in the legs, stretchers, and back posts add a decorative element to the functional design. The rings were burned in on the lathe by holding a piece of thin wire against the spinning blank.

ANATOMY OF A SLAB-AND-STICK CHAIR

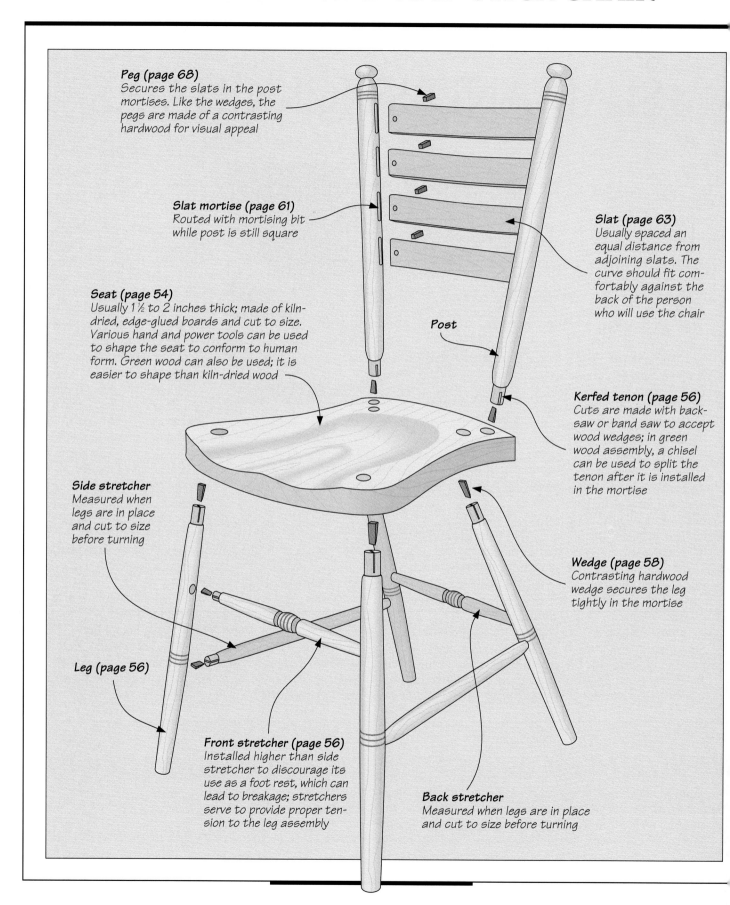

Peg (page 68)
Secures the slats in the post mortises. Like the wedges, the pegs are made of a contrasting hardwood for visual appeal

Slat mortise (page 61)
Routed with mortising bit while post is still square

Slat (page 63)
Usually spaced an equal distance from adjoining slats. The curve should fit comfortably against the back of the person who will use the chair

Seat (page 54)
Usually 1 ½ to 2 inches thick; made of kiln-dried, edge-glued boards and cut to size. Various hand and power tools can be used to shape the seat to conform to human form. Green wood can also be used; it is easier to shape than kiln-dried wood

Post

Kerfed tenon (page 56)
Cuts are made with back-saw or band saw to accept wood wedges; in green wood assembly, a chisel can be used to split the tenon after it is installed in the mortise

Side stretcher
Measured when legs are in place and cut to size before turning

Wedge (page 58)
Contrasting hardwood wedge secures the leg tightly in the mortise

Leg (page 56)

Front stretcher (page 56)
Installed higher than side stretcher to discourage its use as a foot rest, which can lead to breakage; stretchers serve to provide proper tension to the leg assembly

Back stretcher
Measured when legs are in place and cut to size before turning

CUTTING LIST

PIECE	QTY.	TH.	W.	L.	MATERIAL
Seat	1	1¼"	16½"	16½"	cherry
Legs	4	1½"	1½"	18"	cherry
Side stretchers	2	⅞"	⅞"	14¾"	cherry
Back stretcher	1	⅞"	⅞"	13¾	cherry
Front stretcher	1	⅞"	⅞"	12¾"	cherry
Posts	2	1½"	1½"	20"	cherry
Slats	4	⅜"	1¾"	14"	cherry
Pegs and wedges	6 each				contrasting hardwood

Making and using a cutting list

A cutting list records the finished sizes of the wood needed for a project. If you buy plans, a list may be included; otherwise you will have to make your own based on a drawing of the design. Lumber is often sold in board feet. As explained on page 16, 1 board foot is equivalent to a piece of wood 1 inch thick, 12 inches wide, and 12 inches long. Once you have tallied up the number of board feet for all the pieces, you would normally add an extra 20 to 30 percent to account for defects in the wood and waste. Add at least 50 percent for chairs, however, as there is inevitably more waste because the appearance of each element is of critical importance. For the chair project shown in this chapter, which totals roughly 5 board feet, you should order at least 8 board feet and you could quite easily use 10.

Made from green wood, the three-legged milking stool shown at left is a simplified version of the slab-and-stick chair built in this chapter. The rungs are attached to the legs with round mortise-and-tenons, while the legs are joined to the saddle-type seat with a wedged version of the same joint.

PREPARING THE SEAT AND LEGS

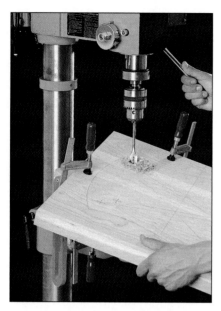

The traditional way to drill mortises in a chair seat for the posts and legs is with a brace and bit, as shown in the following pages, but you can also use a drill press. With either method you will need to drill a compound angle that is raked to the front or back and splayed out to the side. If you are using a drill press, the correct angle of the forward or backward rake is set by tilting the machine's table—or a tilting table jig—to the appropriate angle. Then position the seat blank so the appropriate splay angle reference line (right) is aligned with the drill bit and the column at the back of the machine.

MARKING AND BORING POST AND LEG MORTISES

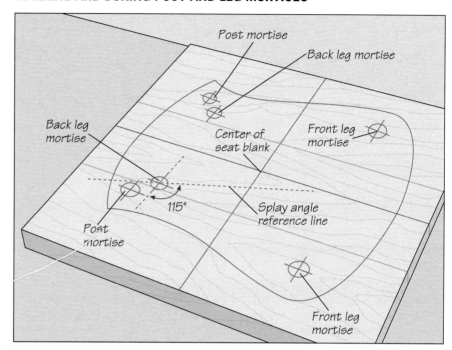

1 Laying out the seat and the mortise outlines
Lay the seat blank face-up on a work surface, mark the center of two adjacent sides and use a carpenter's square to extend the lines to the opposite sides of the blank, bisecting the center of the seat blank. The resulting grid will help you draw a symmetrical outline for the seat. To mark the outline, either use an existing chair and copy it or create your own design using the dimensions in the chart on page 14 as a guideline. In each corner of the seat you will need to mark a mortise for a leg. The back of the seat will also require an extra mortise in each corner for the chair's posts. Use a measuring tape to ensure that the mortises are perfectly symmetrical. You will also need to mark reference lines to help you drill the mortise so the legs and posts will splay out away from the side of the seat at the proper angle. There are no strict guidelines for what this angle should be. Again, use an existing chair as a model. Legs typically flare out by 105° to 115°; posts by 110° to 120°. Use a protractor to mark a reference line through the mortise and extend it toward the center of the seat *(above)*. Repeat this procedure for each mortise.

2 Making a rake angle jig
As well as splaying out, the mortises for the legs and posts must be angled—or raked—toward the front or back of the chair. To help you drill the resulting compound angle you will need the help of a simple jig in addition to the splay angle reference lines you have already drawn on the seat. Use a sliding bevel to mark the rake angle on a piece of scrap stock *(left)*. This angle should be between 10° and 12° from vertical for the front legs and posts, and almost twice that for the back legs. Clamp the stock in a vise and cut along the line. You will need to make a separate jig for each of the different angles you will require for the chair.

Image labels: Post mortise · Back leg mortise · Back leg mortise · Center of seat blank · Front leg mortise · 115° · Splay angle reference line · Post mortise · Front leg mortise

3 Drilling the post mortises

To drill the post mortises, clamp the seat blank to a work surface with a scrap panel underneath to protect the surface and reduce tearout. Next, install a spoon bit in a brace; an auger and a spade bit are suitable alternatives. Line up the drilling guide with the splay angle reference line for one of the post mortises. Then center the bit on the mortise and begin drilling, keeping the bit parallel to the slope of the rake angle jig *(right)*. Repeat to bore the other post mortises.

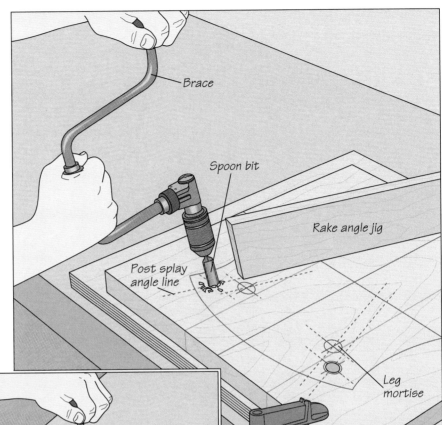

Brace

Spoon bit

Rake angle jig

Post splay
angle line

Leg
mortise

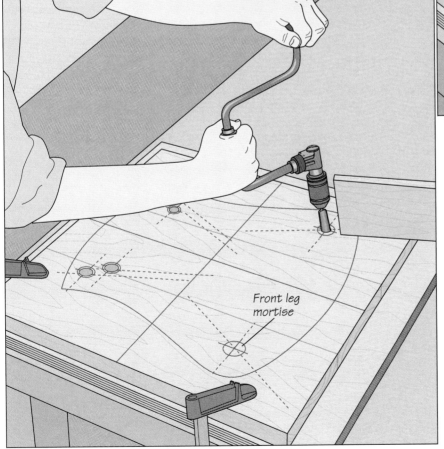

Front leg
mortise

4 Drilling the front and back leg mortises

Use the appropriate rake angle jig to help you drill the back leg mortises, then drill the front leg mortises. In this case, the same guide was used for the front leg mortise as for the posts. Line up the jig with the splay angle reference line and bore the mortise. Then cut out the seat and sculpt it *(page 73)*.

PREPARING THE LEGS AND POSTS

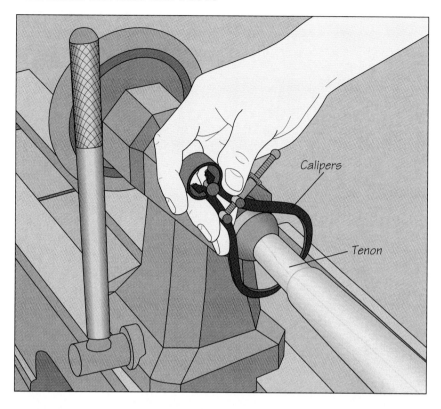

Calipers

Tenon

1 Turning the legs and stretchers on the lathe
Install the square leg stock between centers on your lathe and adjust the tool rest as close as possible to the stock without touching it. Use a roughing gouge to shape the leg, making sure that you keep the bevel rubbing at all times and the tool pointing in the direction of the cut. Then turn the tenon with a parting tool. Turn off the lathe periodically and use calipers to check the diameter of the tenon *(left)*. Then produce the strechers the same way, turning a tenon at each end.

2 Cutting kerfs for wedges in the tenons
Remove the finished leg from the lathe and wrap it in a rag leaving the tenon end exposed, and secure it in a bench vise. The rag will protect the stock from the jaws of the vise. Use a backsaw to slice a kerf in the center of the tenon to a depth of about three-quarters the length of the tenon. Repeat for the other legs and stretchers.

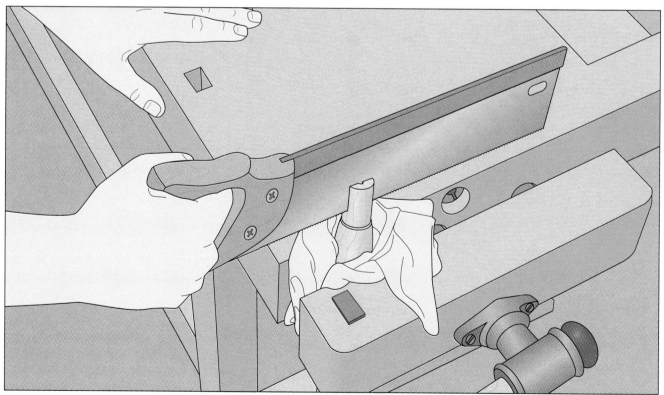

ASSEMBLING LEGS AND STRETCHERS

1 Drilling the stretcher mortises

Stretchers are installed between legs to provide sufficient tension in the leg assembly. Dry assemble the legs in the seat with the kerfs in the tenons perpendicular to the grain of the seat, and position the stretchers. Then cut a piece of scrap stock slightly longer than the distance between two legs. Clamp the wood between the two legs just below the mortise level to serve as a reference for keeping the drill bit horizontal. Place a wood pad between the legs and the clamp jaw, or use clamps with non-marring jaws like those shown at right. Next, install a brad-point bit in an electric drill and wrap a piece of tape around the shaft of the bit to mark the depth that the mortise should be drilled—the length of the stretcher tenon. Holding one leg near the bottom, sight along the horizontal guide and drill the mortise to the proper depth *(right)*. Repeat for the other mortises, readjusting the height of the horizontal guide as required from stretcher to stretcher.

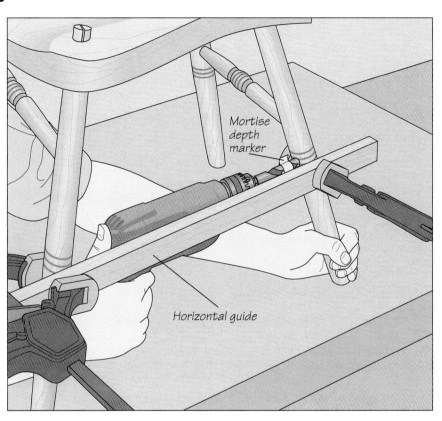

Mortise depth marker

Horizontal guide

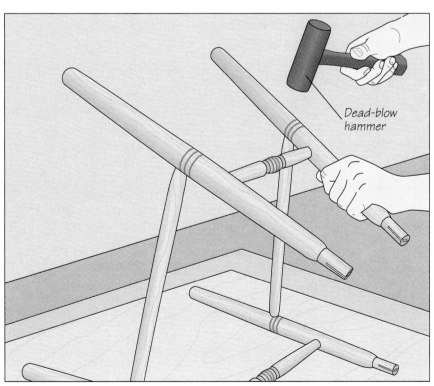

Dead-blow hammer

2 Assembling the stretchers

Clamp a scrap panel, softer than the chair stock, onto a work surface to protect the chair parts. Remove all the legs from the seat. Then, take a leg and put glue in the stretcher mortises and on the mating wedged tenon of the stretcher. Insert the tenon into the mortise and press them firmly together by hand. Repeat this process for each joint until the whole leg-stretcher carriage is assembled. Next, place the assembly on the scrap panel. Holding a leg firmly with one hand, tap the back of each mortise with a dead-blow hammer to seat the tenon fully in the mortise *(left)*. Repeat this procedure for the remaining stretchers. Then proceed quickly to the next step—installing the legs in the seat *(page 58)*—as this must be completed before the glue has cured.

ASSEMBLING THE SEAT AND LEGS

The use of contrasting wood for the wedges in the leg tenons is one way of providing added visual appeal while reinforcing the joint. In the chair shown above, wedges of pau ferro have been hammered into the tenon in a leg made from cherry.

INSTALLING AND SECURING THE LEGS

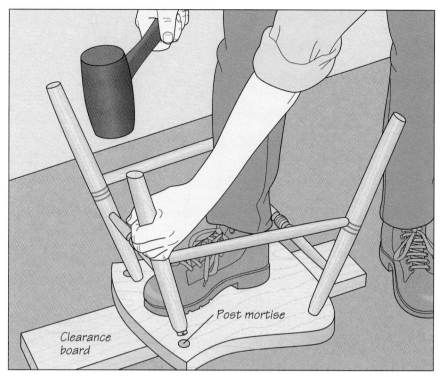

1 Installing the legs in the seat

Place the seat upside-down on a clearance board narrower than the gap between the mortises for the back legs. Insert the leg in its mortises and tap it with a dead-blow hammer until the tenon is wedged tightly in place. Repeat for the remaining legs *(above)*.

2 Wedging the leg tenons

Set the seat upright and trim the tenon ends to slightly above seat level with a flush-cutting saw. To make wedges for the tenons, cut some hardwood pieces on the band saw about 1 inch long and ⅛ inch thick at the base, tapering to a point. Place glue in the kerf and on the wedge, then hammer it in place with a wooden mallet *(right)*. Be careful not to insert the wedge too deeply or it might split the tenon.

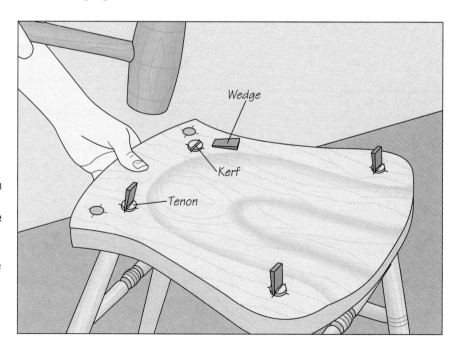

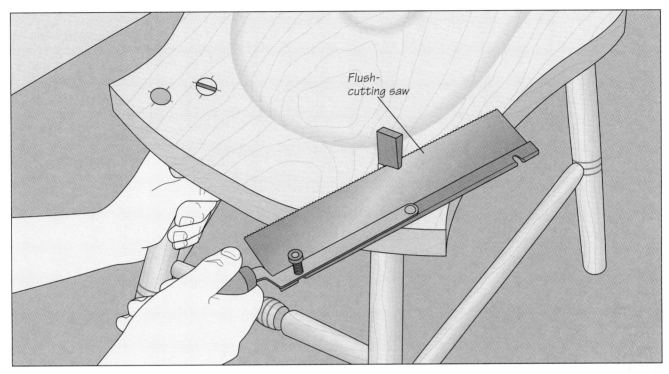

Flush-
cutting saw

3 Trimming the wedges
Holding the chair steady by one leg, trim the wedges and tenons flush to the seat with a flush-cutting saw *(above)*. Finally, sand the surface smooth.

SHOP TIP

Drying green wood tenons in hot sand
If you are making your chair from green wood you need to dry the leg, post, and stretcher tenons before final assembly. The dry wood will then absorb moisture from the mortises and swell when the chair is assembled. At the same time, the seat will shrink around the tenons as it dries, securing those joints together. You can do the job with hot sand. Working outdoors, heat a bucket of fine, dry sand with a propane burner. Insert the legs, posts, and stretchers in the bucket so only the tenons are submerged in the sand. Use a thermometer to monitor the temperature regularly, and adjust the flame to keep the sand between 140° and 160° F; the wood will be burned quickly if subjected to higher temperatures. Leave the tenons in the hot sand for a few hours, rotating them regularly to avoid scorching.

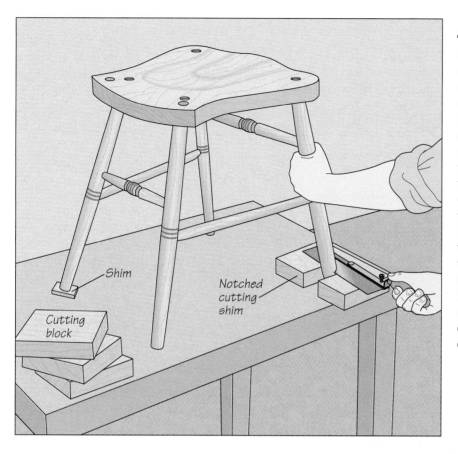

Shim

Notched cutting shim

Cutting block

4 Shimming the chair
The legs of the chair must be shimmed level before trimming them to the desired height. To do this accurately, place the chair on a smooth, level surface. Level the seat from side to side and from front to back by positioning small shims under each leg as required. (Some woodworkers prefer their seats to angle slightly downwards toward the back.) Then decide on the height you want for the seat; 17½ inches is a good guideline, but you can customize a chair to fit the intended user. Make a mark on the chair leg at the point that the leg needs to be cut, then saw four blocks the same thickness as the gap between the mark and the work surface. Notch one of the blocks to fit around a leg. Place the block around the first leg to be cut. Holding the leg firmly with one hand, cut it to size with a flush-cutting saw *(left)*.

5 Trimming the legs to size
Once the first leg is cut to size, remove the notched block and replace it with one of the remaining blocks. Position the notched piece around the next leg and make the cut. Continue in this way until all four legs are cut *(right)*.

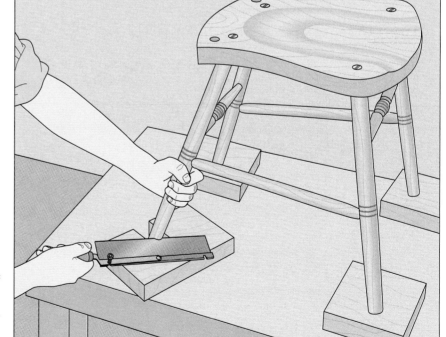

MAKING THE BACK

The slats on the backs of chairs can be left unadorned or embellished with hand-painted motifs or carvings. Here, a scroll saw cuts a decorative design in a slat.

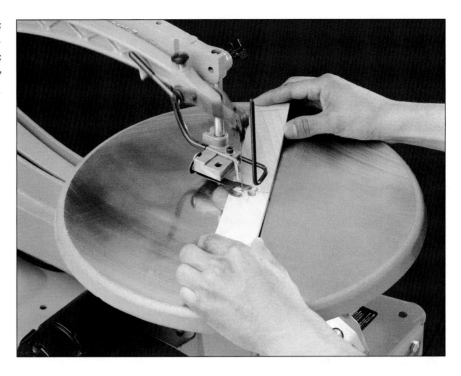

PREPARING THE MORTISES

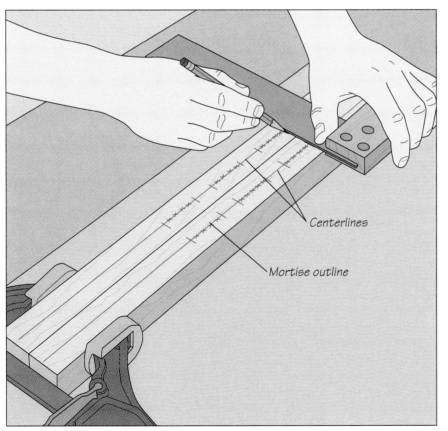

Centerlines

Mortise outline

1 **Marking the mortises**
The first step in making the back is to lay out the mortises for the slats on the posts. Clamp the two pieces of square post stock side-by-side on a work surface. Mark a centerline down the length of each post and use this as a guide for centering the mortises. Then use a piece of slat stock to outline the position of the mortises on one post blank. Determine the position of the slats by taking into account the number of slats, the length of the post, and the spacing between each slat. Use the marked blank as a template for the other post, transferring the finished outline with the aid of a square *(left)*.

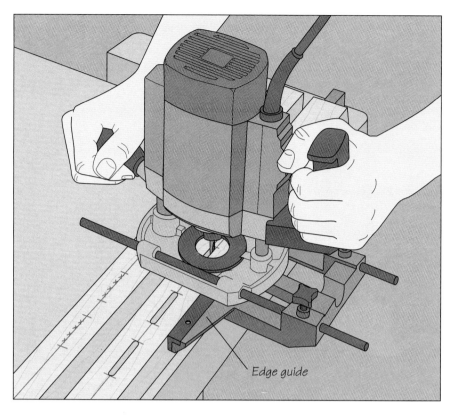

2 Routing the mortises
Secure one of the post blanks between bench dogs. Install a ¼-inch mortising bit in a router equipped with an edge guide. Center the bit over the mortise outline and adjust the edge guide to butt against the stock; use the second post blank to support the router. Make several passes, increasing the cutting depth with each pass until the mortise is completed; a depth of ⅝ inch is typical. Repeat this procedure for all the remaining mortises on the first post *(left)*, then rout the mortises in the second post the same way.

Edge guide

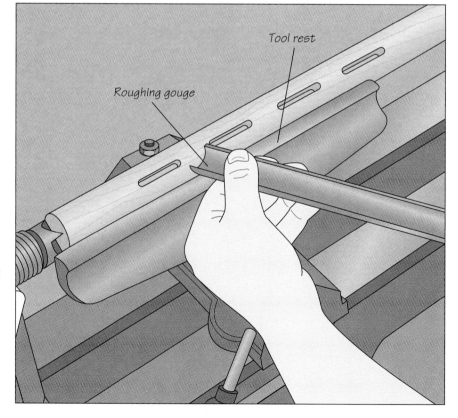

Tool rest

Roughing gouge

3 Turning the post on the lathe
Place the first blank between centers on your lathe and push the tool rest up to the blank as close as possible without touching it. Support the roughing gouge on the rest and, with the blank turning, carefully move the bevel until it touches the stock and the cutting edge starts to remove waste. Continue removing waste up and down the length of the blank until a cylinder is formed *(right)*, with the bevel rubbing and the tool pointing in the direction of the cut. Turn the tenon on the lower end with a parting tool, stopping frequently to test the diameter with calipers. Then cut a kerf in each post for a wedge, as you did for the leg *(page 56)*, ensuring the kerf is perpendicular to the grain of the seat. Repeat the process for the other post blank.

PREPARING THE SLATS

1 Setting up a steaming jig
The slats for the chair back can be bent with the help of a steam box. Build the device from a piece of Schedule 80 ABS piping longer than the length of the slat. Cut the pipe in half and fit one end of each piece to an ABS T-connector. Glue a 1½-inch connector pipe to the T-connector and fasten this to a commercial wallpaper steamer. Build a support structure from 2-by-4s and tilt the pipe slightly with a support block, so any excess water can run out of a drain hole installed in the cap at the lower end of the pipe. The end caps should be the push-on variety to prevent the steamer from becoming over-pressurized. To hold the wood above any condensed water, bore a series of holes along the pipe's length for ⅜-inch zinc-coated machine bolts and nuts, equipped with rubber washers.

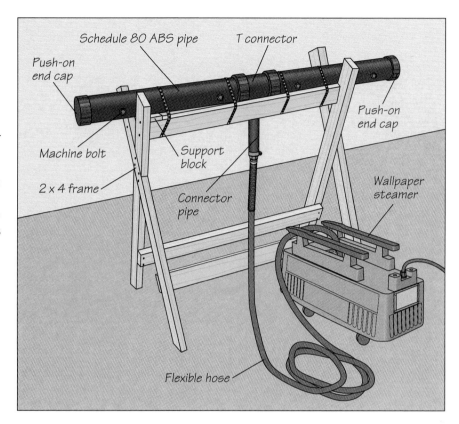

Schedule 80 ABS pipe
T connector
Push-on end cap
Push-on end cap
Machine bolt
Support block
2 x 4 frame
Connector pipe
Wallpaper steamer
Flexible hose

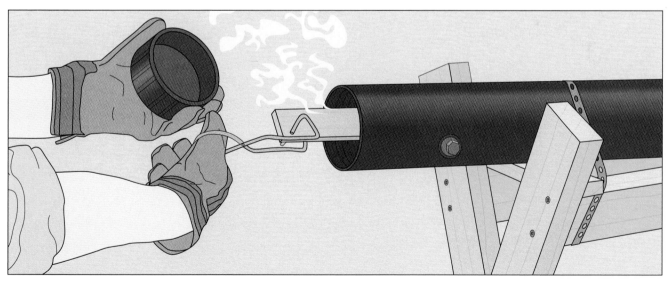

2 Steaming the slats
Turn on the steam source and mark the center of the workpiece to be bent. As soon as steam begins to escape from the drain hole, place the workpiece inside. Close the end cap tightly and let the workpiece steam until it is soft. As a rough guide, steam air-dried lumber for one hour per inch of thickness; half that time for green wood. To avoid scalding your hands, wear work gloves and use tongs to handle the stock (above). The stock can now be bent over a plywood form shaped to the desired curve and then clamped in place until in dries. Or use the jig shown on the following page.

BUILD IT YOURSELF

BENDING FORM

The simple jig shown at right will enable you to bend wood slats to the desired shape once they have been softened by steaming. It consists of two pieces of square stock for a top and bottom support and three equal lengths of dowel. The mortises for the dowels should be centered along the length of the top and bottom supports, one at each end and one in the middle. The distance between the two outside dowels should be slightly less than the span of a slat when it is curved. The dowels should be thick enough to withstand the pressure of the bending—at least ¾ inch thick.

To use the bending form, take each slat out of the steam-bending jig and quickly fit it between the dowels *(right, bottom)*. Wear gloves to avoid scalding your hands. Center the slat against the middle dowel and push the ends behind the outside dowels. Alternate the direction of the slats to equalize the pressure on the jig.

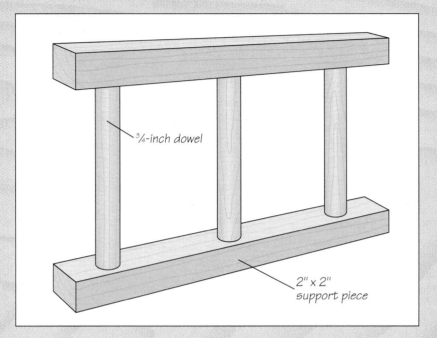

¾-inch dowel

2" x 2" support piece

MEASURING AND PREPARING THE SLATS FOR MORTISES

1 Marking the slats

Let the slats dry in the bending form for a couple of days before cutting them to length. Dry-install the posts in their mortises in the seat, then install a spacer board between the posts to hold them the proper distance apart. Place the top slat behind the posts and align it with its mortises. Mark a line down each end of the slat at the mortise *(right)*. Draw a cutting line ½ inch outside each mark to compensate for the depth of the mortise. Before making the cut, do any shaping work *(step 2)*. This will make it safer for you to feed the slat into the cutter since you will not have to shape to the ends of the stock.

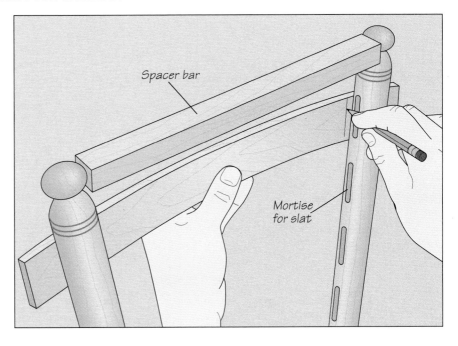

Spacer bar

Mortise for slat

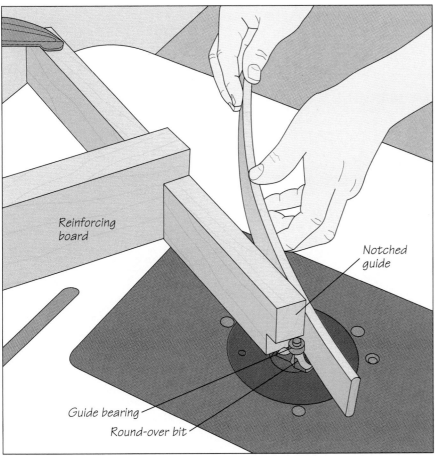

Reinforcing board

Notched guide

Guide bearing

Round-over bit

2 Shaping the slats

The slats can shaped on a table-mounted router. Install a piloted round-over bit in the tool; a ³⁄₁₆-inch bit will work well for ⅜-inch-thick stock. Then prepare a shop-made guide by notching a piece of 1-by-2 to clear the bit. Clamp it in place with the notch directly over the cutter; the edge of the guide should be in line with the router bearing. Reinforce the guide with a piece of 2-by-4 clamped at a 90° angle and notched to fit over the guide. Feed the slat into the cutter, making sure that the stock rests flush against the guide bearing and keeping your fingers well clear of the bit *(left)*.

3 Cutting the slats to length

Once the edges of the slats are shaped, you are ready to cut the pieces to length. Using the band saw, be careful to keep the part of the slat with the cutting line flat on the table while you make the cut *(right)*.

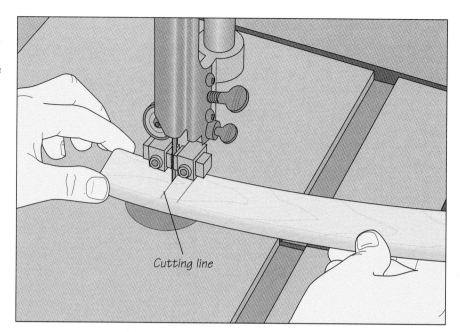

Cutting line

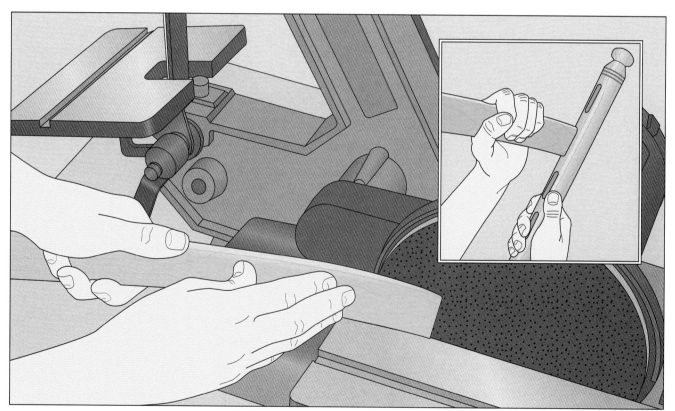

4 Sanding and test-fitting the slats

The ends of the slats need to be sanded to compensate for the angle at which they enter the mortises. Take each trimmed slat and carefully sand down the part of the back face that will fit into the mortise *(above)*. Stop frequently and check to see if the tenon fits all the way into the mortise *(inset)*. A gouge can also be used to cut away the waste until you have a secure fit. You may have to trim the end of the slats slightly to fit into the mortise to allow for the angle of the slat.

INSTALLING THE SLATS AND POSTS

1 **Fitting the slats into the posts**
Put glue in each mortise and on the ends of each slat. Insert the slats into one post, then line them up with the mortises in the other post and press the slats in place *(right)*. Set one of the posts on a scrap panel and give it a few taps from a dead-blow hammer above each mortise to drive the slats in all the way. Flip the assembly over and hammer directly above the mortises in the other post, then proceed quickly to installing the posts in the seat.

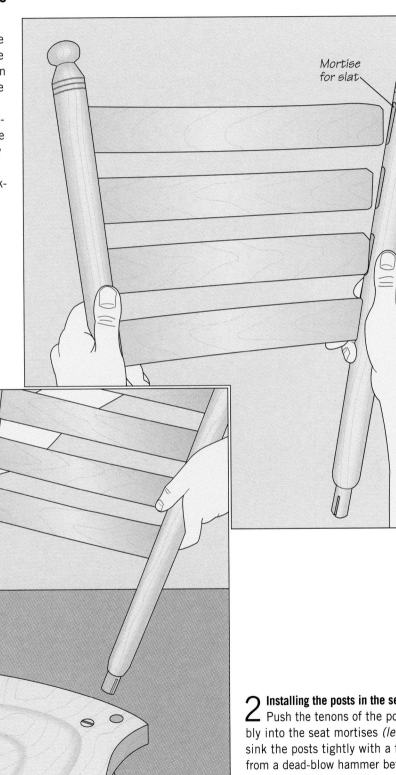

Mortise for slat

Post mortise

2 **Installing the posts in the seat**
Push the tenons of the post assembly into the seat mortises *(left)*. Then sink the posts tightly with a few taps from a dead-blow hammer before securing them with wedges hammered into the tenons *(page 58)*.

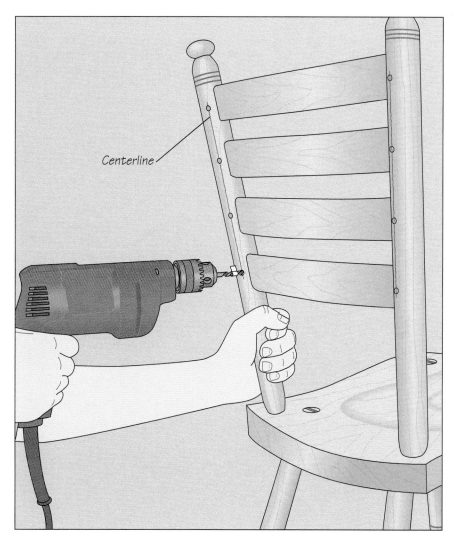

Centerline

3 Preparing the posts and slats for pegs
Once the back is installed, drill the holes for the pegs that will secure the slats to the posts. In an electric drill, install a brad-point bit the same width as your pegs. Then, scribe a line down the inside edge of the posts to line up the peg holes, which should penetrate the post and the slat without exiting from the far side of the posts. Mark the center of each peg hole along this line to indicate the drilling point. Mark the depth on the bit with a piece of masking tape. Use an awl to start the hole. Then place the chair at a comfortable level, grasp a post in one hand, and bore into the post until the tape on the bit touches the stock *(left)*. Repeat this procedure for all the peg holes.

4 Shaping and sharpening the square pegs
Prepare the pegs to secure the slats in the posts. Take the stock (either the same or a contrasting hardwood for a decorative effect) and rip it to size. The sides of the peg should be the same width as the diameter of the hole; use a push stick to keep your fingers well clear of the blade. Then cut the pegs roughly to length on the band saw. Taper one end of each peg slightly with a shop knife to make it easier to hammer into its hole *(right)*.

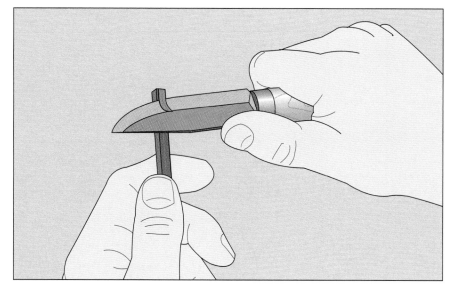

5 Tapping the pegs into the posts
With the chair back clamped securely on a work surface, spread some glue on the tapered end of each peg. Next, position the peg in its hole and tap it with a hammer until you hear a change in tone which will indicate that the peg has bottomed out in the hole. Insert the other pegs the same way.

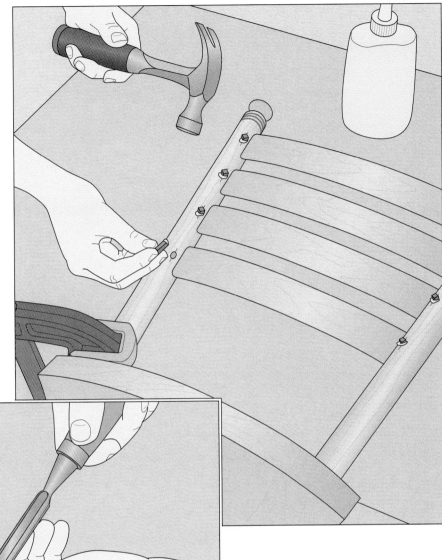

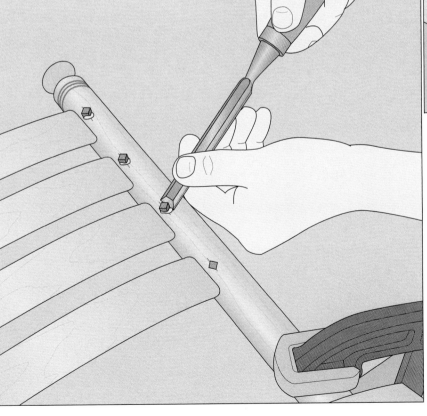

6 Cutting the pegs flush with the posts
With the chair still clamped in place, use a chisel to shave away the pegs a little at a time until they are flush with the post *(left)*. Sand them smooth if necessary.

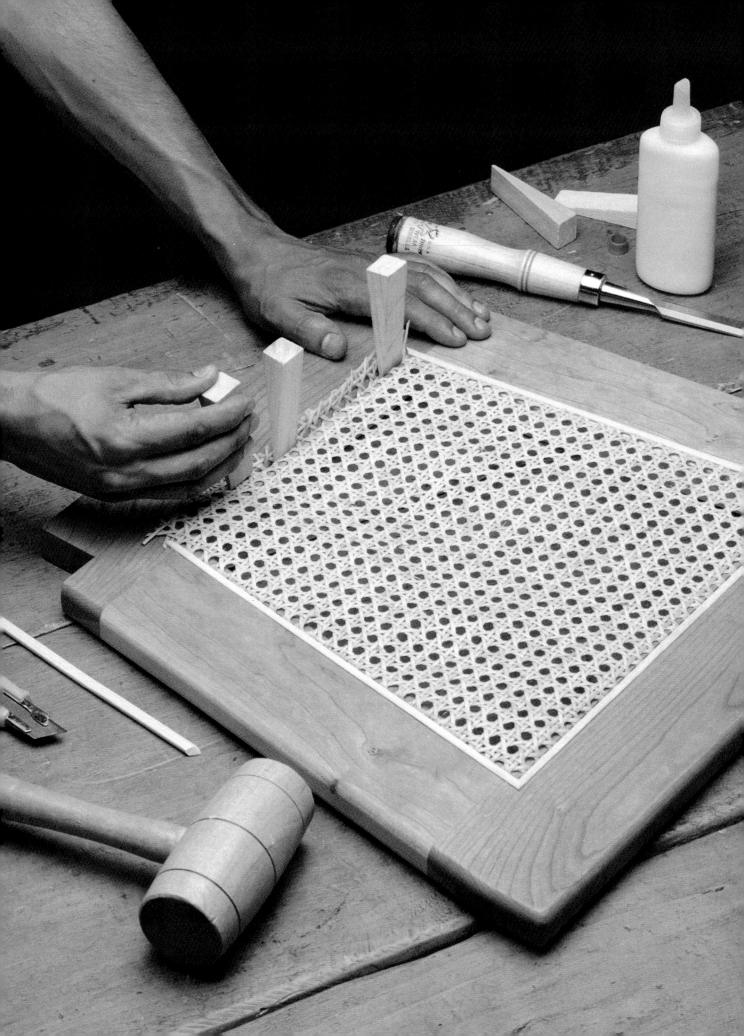

SEATS

The top surface of the wood seat in the frame chair shown above has been sculpted to provide maximum comfort and support for its user.

The seat is the reason for a chair's existence. Backs and arms may be optional—even legs—but every chair needs a seat. Over the centuries, chair makers have settled on many seat styles to suit a variety of applications and uses. In this chapter, you will find techniques for making four types of seats: a solid, sculpted seat; an upholstered seat; a woven cane seat; and a rush seat.

The solid, sculpted seat shown starting on page 73 represents the evolution of what appeared in the earliest chairs and stools as a flat wooden slab mortised to hold three or four legs. The modern solid seat is appropriate for virtually any chair design. Its sculpted surface is ideally suited to frame chairs, as shown in the photo above, and its solidity adds a measure of strength to slab-and-stick chairs *(page 50)*, which use the seat as an integral element of the structure.

The upholstered seat, with its padding and fabric covering *(page 78)*, was a key part of the ornate chairs built in the 17th and 18th Centuries. The comfort and luxurious appearance that it provides makes it a good choice for chairs intended for dining rooms and other formal settings.

The practice of weaving chair seats has a long history. Western chair makers have used cane to make seats for chairs and stools since the 16th Century, while the Egyptians were making rush seats more than 3,000 years ago. Cane and rush seats remain popular, and the techniques and materials for weaving them are virtually unchanged. Cane strands are cut from the bark of the Asian rattan plant and are available in various widths. Although caning a seat requires few tools *(page 83)*, it is a time-consuming process that demands patience. Weaving a typical cane seat can take as long as 12 hours.

A less time-consuming option is prewoven caning, which is wedged into a groove around the seat frame, as shown in the photo on page 70.

Today, rush seats are generally woven with twisted kraft paper rather than natural rush—except on reproduction pieces. Sold in various widths and colors, fiber rush seats are very durable. Rushing a seat, as shown on page 90, is an easier technique to master than caning, and is an excellent way to span the seat frame of a stick chair.

Although woven seats are intended to last a long time, they usually do not last as long as the chair itself. The chair being rewoven on page 90, for example, is more than a hundred years old. Before reweaving an old cane seat, be sure to remove any fasteners from the edges of the seat frame.

Prewoven cane is glued into a seat frame, held in place temporarily by wooden wedges. Before installation, the cane is soaked for two hours in warm water. It is then stretched tightly over the seat and wedged into grooves routed in the inside edges of the frame. The cane is secured permanently, one side at a time, by a reed spline. In the photo at left, splines have been glued in the grooves on three sides of the seat. As each spline is installed, the excess cane is cut away. (See page 120.)

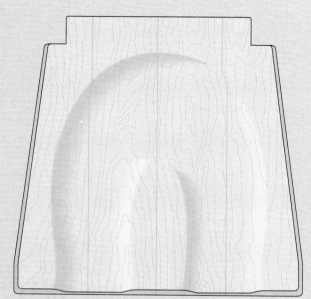

Sculpted seat (page 73)
*A wood slab made from boards edge-glued together;
suitable for any chair, particularly one needing solid
seat support. The surface is usually contoured to
suit the chair's design and the needs of its user.
Normally fastened to the top edge of the seat rails
or mortised to receive legs and posts.*

Upholstered seat (page 78)
*A plywood base with padding covered by fabric;
typically recessed within the seat rails.*

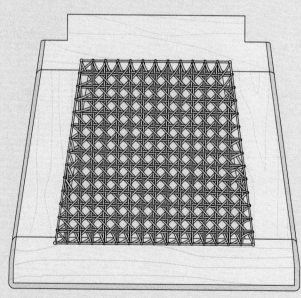

Cane seat (page 83)
*Seat consists of a frame joined by mortise-and-
tenon or plate joints. Cane is hand-woven in individual strands; prewoven cane can also be glued
into a groove routed around the seat. Seat is usually fastened to the seat rails.*

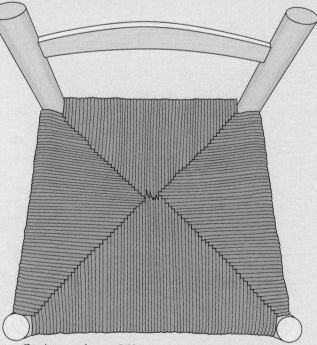

Rush seat (page 90)
*Strands of fiber or kraft paper are woven
across the posts and rails of a stick chair;
provides a sturdy seat that is simple and
inexpensive to apply and renew.*

SCULPTED SEATS

The sculpted seat design featured in this section is intended for a frame chair. (If you are making a seat for a slab-and-stick chair, see page 54. The procedure for sculpting the seat, as shown on pages 75 and 76, is the same for both types of chairs.)

Begin by making a seat blank that is a few inches larger than the seat frame by edge-gluing pieces of 1- to 1 ½-inch-thick solid stock; for a typical chair, a 20-inch-square blank should be sufficient. Arrange the boards so that the grain of the seat will run from front to back.

A sculpted seat blank is test-fitted against the rear legs of the frame chair shown at left. The first step in sizing the blank involves positioning it on the seat rails and outlining the notches that must be cut out for the rear legs. For the width of the notches, add ⅟₁₆ inch of clearance between the blank and the legs to allow for wood movement. For the depth, measure from the front of the leg to about ⅛ inch beyond the back seat rail and add the overhang for the front. Once you have marked the cutting lines on the top of the blank, use a try square to extend them to the underside.

PREPARING THE SEAT

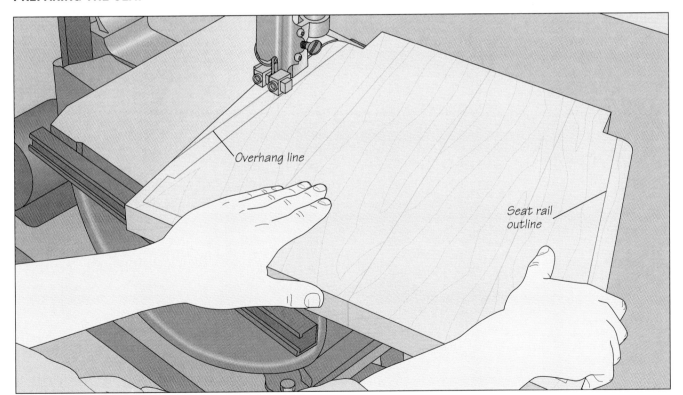

Overhang line

Seat rail outline

1 Cutting the seat blank to size
Outline the notches for the rear legs on the blank *(photo, above)* and cut them on your band saw. Then position the blank on the seat frame and outline the outside of the frame and the front legs on the underside of the blank. Turn the blank over and mark a second set of lines parallel to and ½ inch outside the first set of lines. These will be your cutting lines; the seat will overhang the frame by ½ inch. Round the corner between the rear legs and the sides, then saw along the cutting lines, starting with one side, continuing to the front and finishing with the second side *(above)*.

2 Jointing the edges of the seat

Use your jointer to remove the saw marks left on the edges on both sides of the seat. Adjust the machine for a shallow cut and make a pass on each edge, keeping the edge flat on the jointer tables and the face flush against the fence *(right)*. To ensure smooth results, feed the seat so that the knives will cut with the wood grain—in this case, with the front of the seat leading and the back trailing. Do not try to smooth the front and back ends of the seat on the jointer; the knives will tear at the end grain. Instead, use a sander.

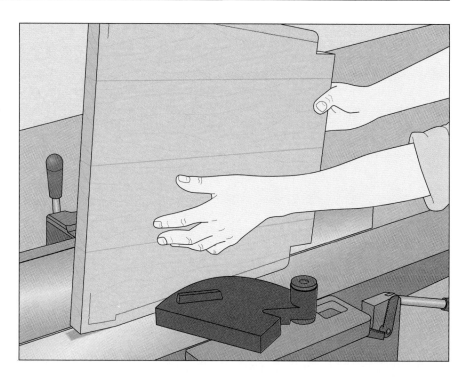

Fence

Bit guard

3 Rounding over the edges of the seat

For the sake of comfort and appearance, round over the side edges and the front end of the seat. Install a ⅜-inch round-over bit in a router and mount the tool in a table. Fashion a guard for the bit and a fence for the workpiece to ride against on the infeed side of the table, as shown above. Screw the guard and fence together and clamp them to the table. Hold the seat flat on the table and flush against the fence as you feed each edge into the bit *(above)*. Then turn the seat over and round over the edges on the other side the same way. Do not shape the back end of the seat; it should remain square. Smooth the end and edges with sandpaper, working with progressively finer grits.

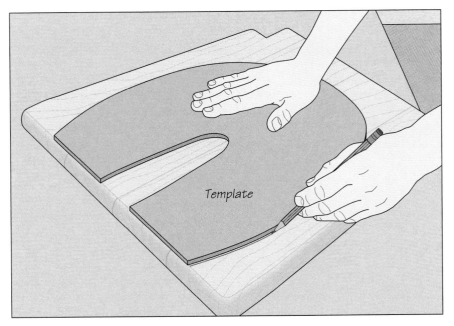

4 Outlining the shape of the seat's top

Mark the outline of the shape of the seat's top surface on a hardboard or plywood scrap and cut it out as a template. The outline should typically be rounded at the back and taper toward the front, as shown at left. Place the template on the seat and transfer the outline to its top surface.

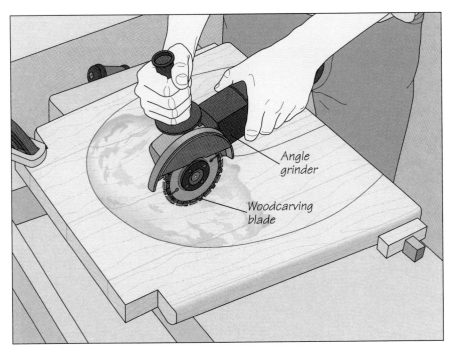

5 Shaping the seat top

Secure the seat on a workbench with its top surface up, using clamps and bench dogs to hold it steady and wood pads to protect the stock. You can cut the recess by hand with an adze, or with an angle grinder equipped with a special woodcarving blade, as shown above. The chainsaw-like blade is well suited to removing waste wood quickly and in a controlled fashion from a broad surface. Holding the grinder with a firm two-handed grip, sweep it from side to side within the outline to excavate the recess in a series of shallow cuts. At the back of the outline, work across the grain *(above, left)*; move the grinder along the grain at the front of the seat *(above, right)*. The recess should be a little deeper at the back and at the front than in the middle. Periodically test the comfort of the seat by sitting on it and check the depth of the recess by placing a straightedge across the seat and measuring the gap between the edge and the seat. As a rule of thumb, do not cut deeper than halfway through the seat's thickness.

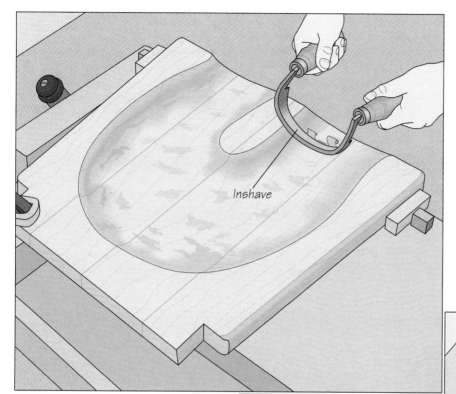

Inshave

6 Completing the recess
To remove any ridges or uneven spots left in the recess by the adze or angle grinder, use a carving gouge or an inshave, as shown at left. Holding the inshave with both handles, pull the tool towards you to slice away thin shavings of waste wood *(left)*. Try to work the inshave with the grain as much as possible. Should you need to pull it across the grain, be careful to avoid cutting into the edges of the recess.

7 Smoothing the seat
To sand the surface of the seat quickly, use a random-orbit sander with a foam pad installed between the sanding disk and the sander's platen. Start with a rough-grit sanding disk, trying to reach all areas of the recess *(right)*. Before moving on to finer-grit disks, inspect the recess for any uneven spots and smooth them with the inshave. Sand the seat until the surface is uniformly smooth.

INSTALLING THE SEAT

1 Drilling pilot holes in the rails
Since a solid chair seat for a frame chair is typically fastened to the top of the seat rails, you must drill the screw holes in the rails before assembling the chair. Mark three drilling points along the bottom edge of each rail, one in the middle and near each end. Bore the holes in two steps, starting with a brad-point bit slightly larger than the shank of the screws you will be using. If you are using your drill press, hold the rail on the table and drill a hole through the workpiece at each marked point *(right)*. Once all the clearance holes are drilled, install a bit slightly larger than the screw heads and bore holes that overlap the clearance holes, drilling only deep enough to recess the screw heads.

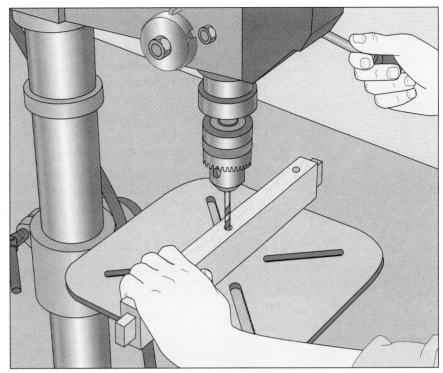

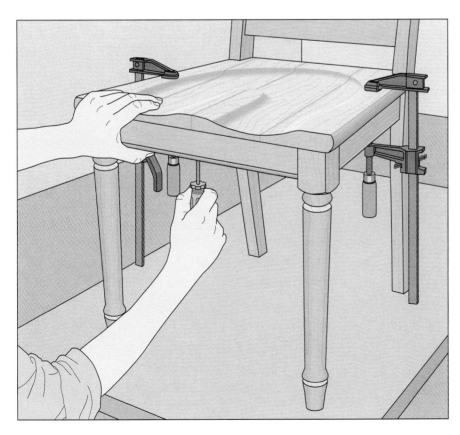

2 Fastening the seat to the rails
Once the chair has been glued up, set it on a work surface and clamp the seat in position on the seat rails. The clamps shown at left have plastic pads on the jaws to protect the stock. Holding the the seat and rails together snugly, drive the screws from underneath through the clearance holes and into the seat.

UPHOLSTERED SEATS

Apart from extra comfort, one benefit of an upholstered seat is that it can be recessed in the seat rails, as in the frame chair shown at left. This feature allows the rails to frame the pattern of the fabric covering the seat.

MAKING THE SEAT

1 Preparing the seat base
Make a plywood or hardboard template of the top surface of the chair's seat rails. If the seat will rest within the rails make the template ¼ inch smaller than the seat frame to allow for the recess; if the seat will lie on top of the rails size the template the same as you would a solid sculpted seat *(page 73)*. Trace the outline from the template onto a piece of ½- or ¾-inch plywood and cut it out on your band saw. The plywood will be the seat base. Then insert a large-diameter bit in your drill press and bore several holes through the base *(right)*. The holes will allow air to escape from the foam padding when the seat is sat on and compressed.

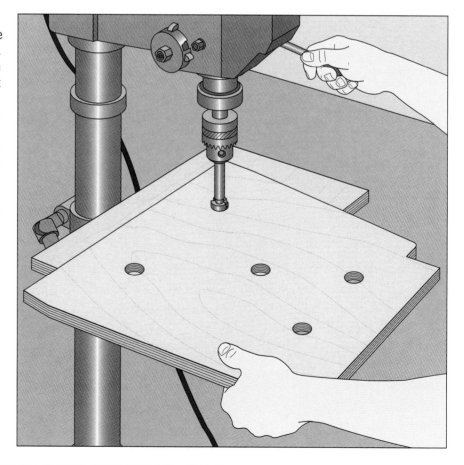

2 **Gluing the foam padding to the seat base**
Buy a piece of 1½-inch-thick foam padding from a craft supply or handware store and cut it using a sharp knife to fit over the seat base. A utility knife with a retractable blade will work well for slicing through thick padding. To install the padding, coat the top of the seat base and the underside of the padding with contact cement, let the adhesive dry according to the manufacturer's directions and press the two pieces together *(right)*.

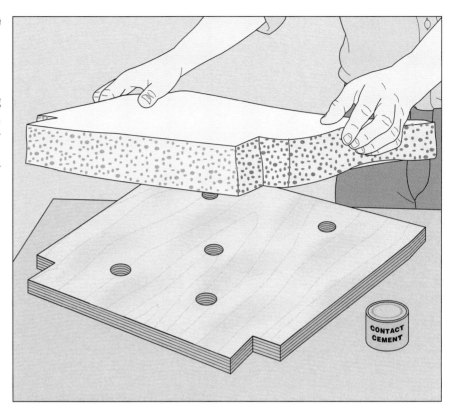

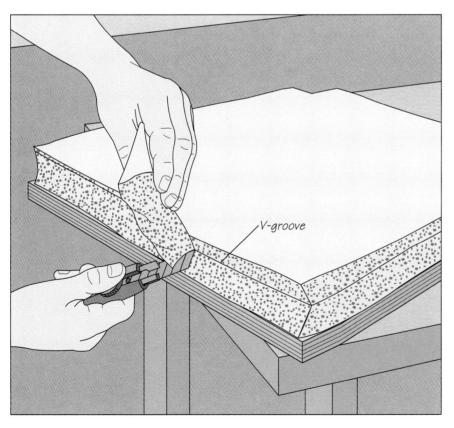

3 **Trimming the padding**
To enable the padding to fold and round over when the fabric covering is applied, cut a V groove into the edges of the foam. Cut into the top of one edge with the utility knife at a 45° angle, penetrating halfway through the pad's thickness. Then run the knife to an adjoining corner, cutting one-half of the groove. Repeat along the bottom of the edge, removing the strip of padding as you go. Cut the groove the same way on the remaining edges of the padding *(left)*.

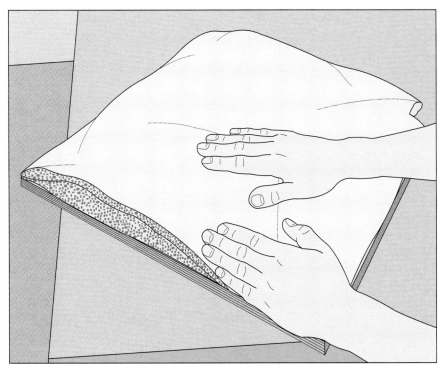

4 **Gluing down the edges of the padding**
Once all the grooves have been cut into the padding, the edges are ready to be folded down. Apply contact cement to the top and bottom of the grooves, let the adhesive dry, and fold the two parts together *(left)*. Apply hand pressure all around the edges of the padding to ensure uniform and complete contact, then use the knife to trim away any padding overhanging the seat base.

5 **Installing underlay**
Before fastening the fabric covering to the seat, you need to attach a piece of cloth underlay to the base. This will serve as a barrier between the upholstery fabric and the padding, preventing the fabric from adhering to the foam. An old bedsheet is ideal material for the underlay; cut a section several inches larger than the top of the seat. To install it, set the underlay on a work surface and center the seat padded-side down on top. Fold the material over the front of the seat and staple it to the base. Staple the underlay at the back, pulling the material tight and making sure the fabric is neat in the notches for the rear legs. Finally, fasten the underlay over the sides *(right)*. Trim away excess material with scissors.

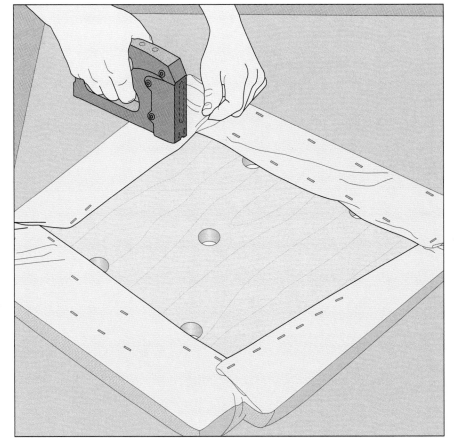

6 Attaching the fabric covering

Cut a piece of fabric to cover the seat and install it as you would the underlay *(page 80)*. Since the fabric is the only visible layer of the upholstered seat, take special care to fold and staple the fabric neatly at the corners *(right)*. Once the fabric is attached to the base, fasten the seat to the corner blocks in the seat frame, driving the screws from underneath. If the seat will be recessed in the frame, remember to prepare the seat rails *(step below)* before proceeding with the final assembly of the chair.

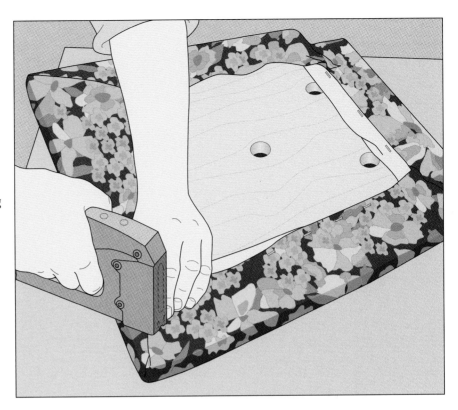

PREPARING THE SEAT RAILS FOR A RECESSED SEAT

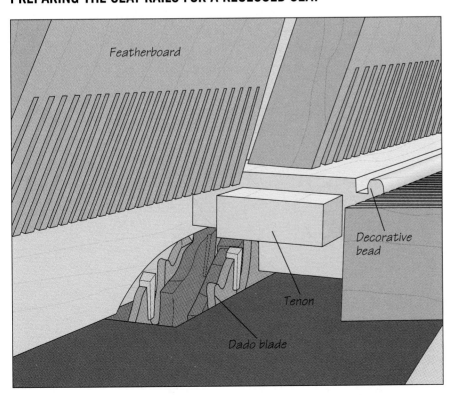

Featherboard

Decorative bead

Tenon

Dado blade

1 Rabbeting the seat rails

Install a dado blade on your table saw, adjusting it slightly wider than the thickness of the seat base. Set the cutting height to about one-half of the rail thickness. (The rail shown has a decorative bead cut into its outside face.) Next, install a wooden auxiliary fence on the rip fence and notch it with the dado head. To support the rails, use three featherboards, clamping one to the fence on each side of the blades and a third to the table in line with the dado head. Feed the rails inside-face down, running the top edge along the fence *(left)*. Complete each pass with a push stick. Once all the rabbets are sawn, you can glue up the chair.

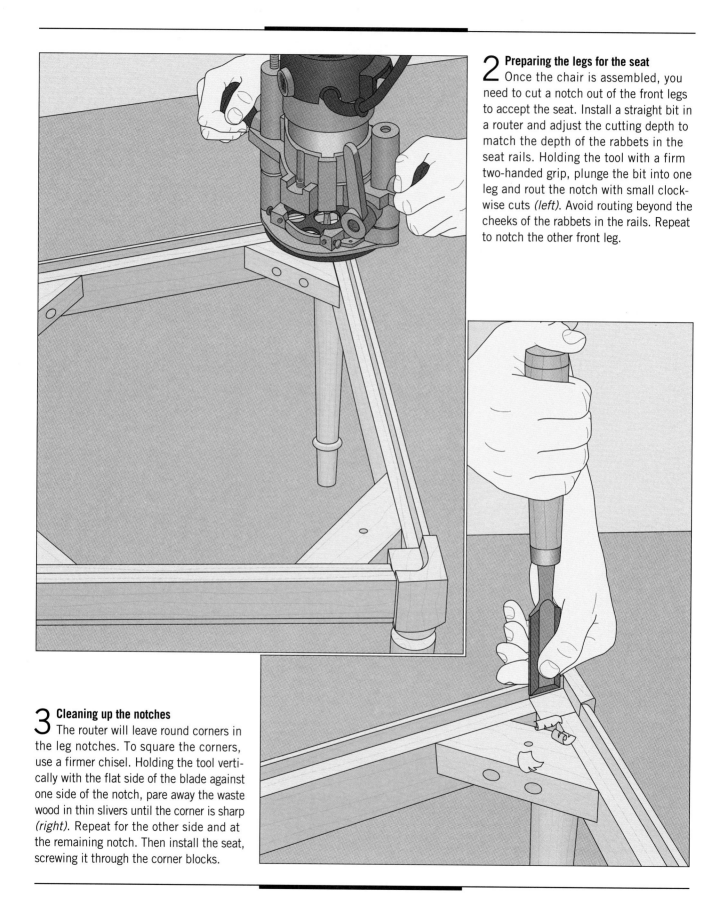

2 Preparing the legs for the seat

Once the chair is assembled, you need to cut a notch out of the front legs to accept the seat. Install a straight bit in a router and adjust the cutting depth to match the depth of the rabbets in the seat rails. Holding the tool with a firm two-handed grip, plunge the bit into one leg and rout the notch with small clockwise cuts *(left)*. Avoid routing beyond the cheeks of the rabbets in the rails. Repeat to notch the other front leg.

3 Cleaning up the notches

The router will leave round corners in the leg notches. To square the corners, use a firmer chisel. Holding the tool vertically with the flat side of the blade against one side of the notch, pare away the waste wood in thin slivers until the corner is sharp *(right)*. Repeat for the other side and at the remaining notch. Then install the seat, screwing it through the corner blocks.

CANE SEATS

This section of the chapter will show you how to cane a chair seat by hand. Although the process is laborious—it can take up to 12 hours to weave a seat for a typical chair—the result is both sturdy and elegant. As shown below, the first step involves making a frame and fastening it to the seat rails. The cane is anchored to this frame.

Cane is usually sold in bundles called hanks, made of 10- to 20-foot lengths totaling 1000 feet. This is usually enough for about four chair seats. The chart on page 84 shows the various widths of cane available and the diameter of the holes you need to drill through the frame to accept the strands. The only other supplies required are special wooden pegs to hold the strands of cane in the holes as you weave them, but golf tees will do.

There are a few rules you should follow as you cane a seat. To keep the strands flexible, keep two or three in a bucket of warm water for 15 to 20 minutes, replacing each one as it is used. Some people add glycerine to make the cane easier to thread. Should a length dry and become brittle as you weave it, you can sponge a bit of water on it. Always keep the cane's glossy-side up. Do not allow the cane to twist, especially under the seat frame or in the holes. Also, the cane can only be woven in one direction; otherwise, it will catch and break. Run a fingernail along the glossy side and you will notice a bump every foot or so. Each bump is a leaf node. Your nail will catch on the nodes in one direction, but not in the other. Weave the cane in the direction that allows you to pull the leaf nodes through the holes without catching. When a length of cane comes to an end, peg it in a hole, trim it to leave an excess of about 5 inches, and start a new length up through the adjacent hole.

Chair caning traces its origins to medieval China. It was introduced in America in the second half of the 17th Century and has experienced a revival since the 1940s. The process is time-consuming but not difficult to master. The result is a chair seat that can last decades.

MAKING THE CANING FRAME

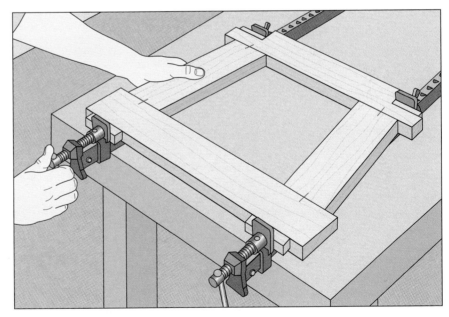

1 Making the frame
Use your seat template *(page 26)* to determine the dimensions of the caning frame. Each of the four pieces should be about 3½ inches wide and can overhang the front and side rails of the seat rails by approximately ½ inch, if you wish. Cut notches for the rear legs in the back frame piece, then glue the pieces together, using a mortise-and-tenon or biscuit joint at each corner. When clamping, protect your stock with wood pads *(above)*.

CANE SIZE	ACTUAL WIDTHS	METRIC WIDTH	HOLES DIAMETER	HOLES CENTER TO CENTER
Super Fine		2 mm	1/8"	3/8"
Fine Fine		2.25 mm	3/16"	1/2"
Fine		2.5 mm	3/16"	5/8"
Narrow Medium		2.75 mm	1/4"	3/4"
Medium		3 mm	1/4"	3/4"
Common		3.5 mm	5/16"	7/8"

2 Preparing the frame for caning

Once the glue has cured, cut the frame to final size, then mark a line all around the frame ½ inch from the inside edges. Add a mark along the line in the middle of the front and back rails. Then refer to the chart above to find the spacing and diameter of the holes required for the width of cane you are using. Mark the holes along the line, adjusting the spacing, if necessary, to ensure that the holes will be equidistant. Then install a brad-point bit of the correct diameter in your drill press. Set the frame on the table, align a corner mark under the bit, and clamp a board to the table flush against the edge of the frame as a guide. Bore a hole through the frame at each mark, holding the stock against the edge guide *(right)*. Once all the holes are drilled, twist a piece of sandpaper into a cone and smooth the holes so that there will be no sharp edges that might tear the cane.

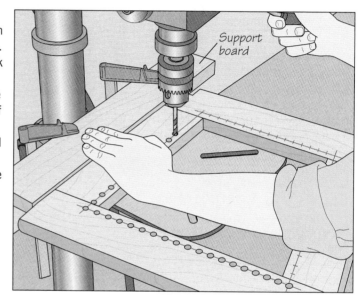

WEAVING THE CANE

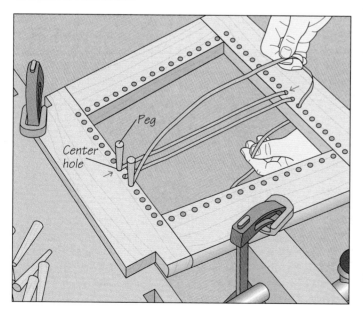

1 Weaving the first vertical rows

Clamp the caning frame to a workbench so that the holes are unobstructed. Then take a length of cane from your bucket and feed it from above into the center hole in the back frame piece. Leave about 5 inches hanging below the frame and insert a peg into the hole to secure the strand. Now bring the strand across the frame and through the top of the center hole in the front piece; pull it fairly taut and peg it. (You should be able to deflect the strand an inch or so.) Pass the strand up through the adjacent hole on the front piece and bring it across to the back piece, feeding it down from the top into the hole next to where you started. Continue in this fashion *(left)*, moving one hole sideways and up and then across the frame, always transferring the peg from the last hole. Leave the first peg in place as well as any peg securing the end or start of a strand.

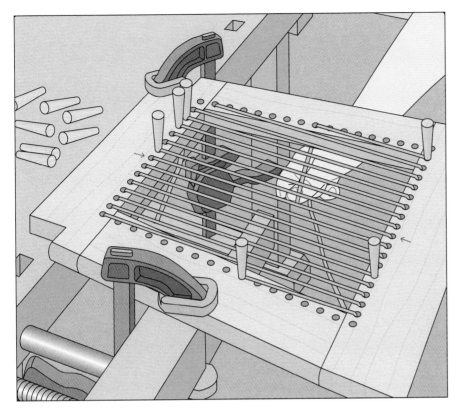

2 Keeping the rows parallel

If your caning frame is trapezoidal rather than square, as in the example shown here, you will have to peg the strands in a hole in the side piece, rather than the front or back, as you reach the side of the frame. This will keep the last row parallel to the preceding ones. When you get to the side piece, choose the appropriate hole and feed the caning into it as described in the step 1 *(left)*. Once this is done, return to the hole adjacent to where you started and weave the cane toward the opposite side. Remember to peg the cane at the beginning and end of each strand, leaving about 5 inches hanging below the frame.

3 Installing the first horizontal rows

Once the first set of vertical rows has been installed, move on to the first horizontal row. Start with the first hole in one side piece at the back of the frame. Remove the peg from the hole if there is one, then feed the cane up through the hole and insert a peg to secure the strand. Pull the strand over the frame and the horizontal rows already in place, and secure the cane into the first hole in the opposite side piece, using a peg. Continue to weave horizontal rows as you did the vertical rows *(right)*, working from the back toward the front of the frame.

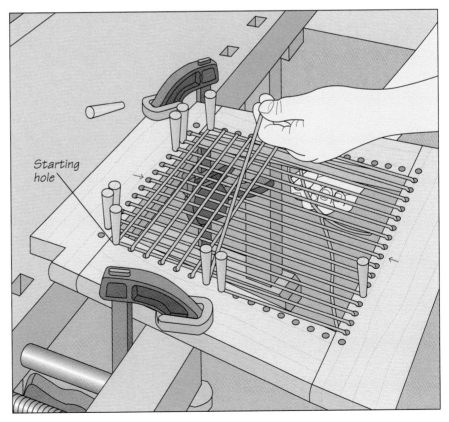

Starting hole

4 Adding the second vertical rows

Weave the second vertical row as you did the first, passing the cane over all the strands in place. However, instead of starting at the middle of the back rail, begin with the last hole you pegged in the first vertical row in the lefthand side of the seat frame. Then, weave the cane from this point *(right)* toward the opposite side, aligning the strands slightly to the right of the first set of vertical strands.

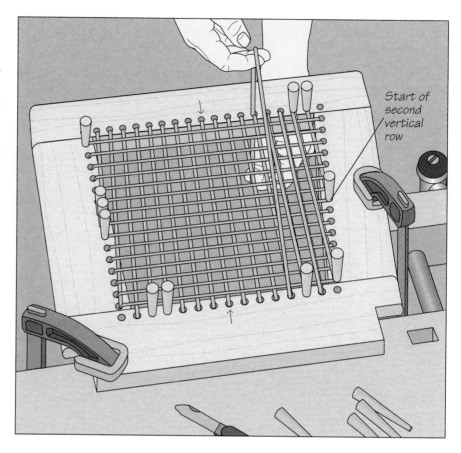

Start of second vertical row

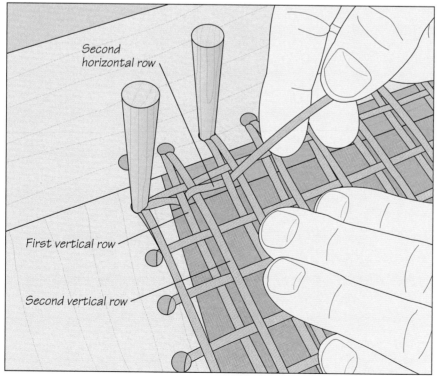

Second horizontal row

First vertical row

Second vertical row

5 Weaving the second horizontal rows

Now the weaving begins with the second horizontal row. Start with the same hole in which you started the first horizontal row and peg the strand in place. Then, weave the cane under the first vertical row and over the second one, positioning the cane beside the first horizontal row *(left)*. Continue weaving in this way until you reach the seat front, and peg the last strand in place.

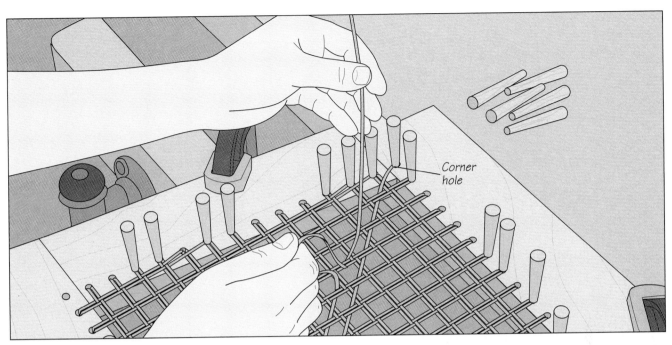

6 Weaving the first diagonal rows

Peg a length of cane in one of the corner holes at the back of the frame. Pass the cane over the horizontal strands and under the vertical strands to the immediate right *(above)*. Continue until you reach the opposite corner hole. Then pass the strand up through the hole in the front frame piece next to the corner hole and work your way toward the back of the seat, weaving the cane under the vertical rows and over the horizontal ones *(right)*. Continue weaving diagonal rows this way until you reach the other corner hole in the front of the seat, making sure that all the rows are parallel. Now, return to the hole in the back of the chair frame next to where you started the diagonal rows and repeat the process, working in the opposite direction.

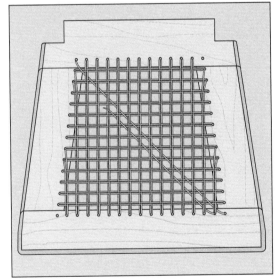

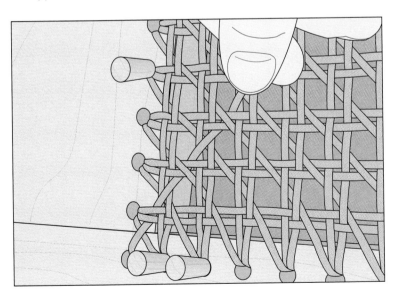

7 Weaving the second diagonal rows

Start the second diagonal weave in the left-hand corner hole in the front of the chair frame. This time, feed the cane over the vertical rows and under the horizontal one *(left)*. Complete the rows as in step 6.

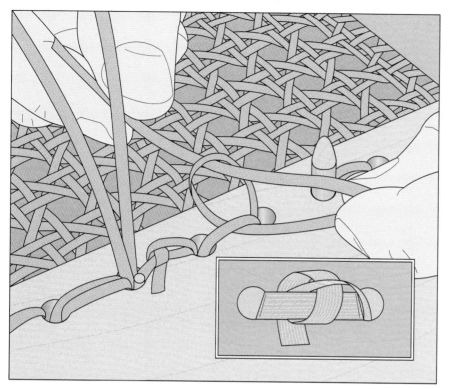

8 Tying off the loose ends of cane
Once the second diagonal row is done, it is time to secure the loose strands hanging under the frame. Turn the seat frame over and use the double-loop knot shown in the inset to secure each strand. To tie this knot, slip a loose strand under an adjacent strap of cane. Then feed it through the loop you just created *(left)*, pass it under the strap again and cinch it tight. Trim the remaining portion, leaving a ½-inch-long tip.

9 Appplying the binder cane
Once the weaving is done and all the ends have been tied-off, apply a strip of binder cane around the perimeter of the seat to give it a neat and finished appearance. Binder cane is usually one or two sizes larger than the cane used for the weave. Pass the end of the binder cane down through the left-back corner hole and peg it in place. Lay the binder cane across the row of holes in the back frame piece, then use a length of weaving cane smaller than the one you used for the seat to anchor the binder cane. Tie loops over the binder cane by passing the weaving strand up through the first hole adjacent to the corner, over the binder cane, and back down through the same hole *(right)*. Move on to the next hole in the back of the seat frame and repeat, continuing until you reach the corner hole at the end of the piece. Trim off the excess length of binder cane and use new lengths along the remaining frame pieces.

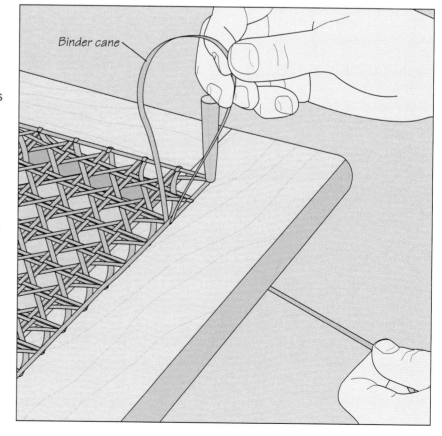

Binder cane

10 Pegging the corners
Once all the binder cane is installed, tie off the ends of the weaving cane you used to anchor it. At each corner, pull the binder cane taut and temporarily tap a peg into the corner hole. Mark the peg at the point where it meets the top of the frame piece, remove the peg and trim it at the mark. Spread a little glue on the sides of the peg and tap it in place with a hammer *(left)*. Then trim the peg flush with a chisel.

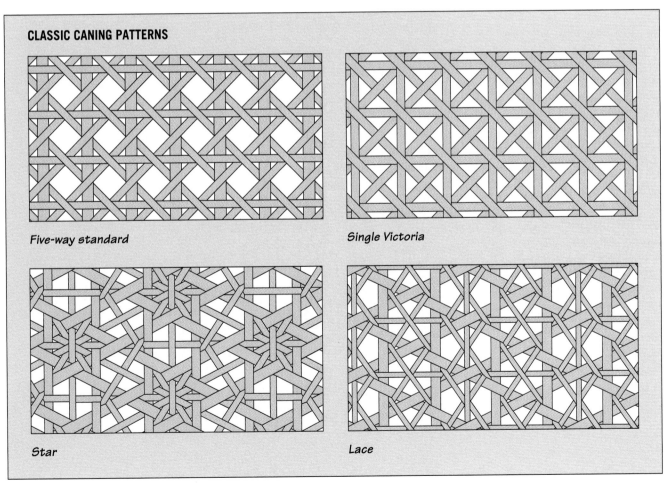

CLASSIC CANING PATTERNS

Five-way standard

Single Victoria

Star

Lace

RUSH SEATS

A simple rush seat can give a charming old chair, like the one shown above, a new lease on life.

Traditionally, rush for chair seats was made of twisted cattail leaves. Nowadays, it is more common to use a tough-grade, fiber paper twisted into long strands, known as "fiber rush." It is sold by the pound and comes in three sizes: 4/32 inch for fine work, 5/32 inch for most chairs, and 6/32 inch for larger pieces and patio furniture. Craft supply dealers are usually good sources of advice for the appropriate size and the amount of rush needed for a particular project. Before applying rush to a seat frame, make sure the glue used to assemble the chair has cured completely. The rush will exert a moderate amount of tension to the joints when it is installed.

Rushing a chair seat is simpler than caning since it involves repeating a single technique all around the seat frame. Rush works best on chairs with square seats and with front legs that extend slightly above the seat rails. This additional height will support the weave as it is wrapped around the corners. Seats that are not square can still have rush seats, as long as you lay down a few preliminary weaves across the side and front rails to create parallel sides, as shown below.

Before starting, spray the individual lengths of rush with water to keep them pliable. Always pull the rush tightly around the rails and keep adjacent rows as close together as possible.

RUSHING A CHAIR SEAT

1 Bridging the front rail

If the seat rails do not form a square, you will need to use rush to create a square frame. Measure the difference in length between the longer and shorter rails—in this case, the front and back rails—and divide your measurement in half. Measure your result along the front rail from each of the front legs and make a mark on the rail. Tack a length of dampened rushing that is about twice the length of the front rail to the inside of a side rail about 2 inches from the front leg. Now loop the rush around the front rail from underneath, then around the side rail from underneath. Bring the rush across the front rail and loop it around the other side rail and the front rail in the same manner *(right)*. Holding the rush taut, tack it to the side rail opposite the first tack.

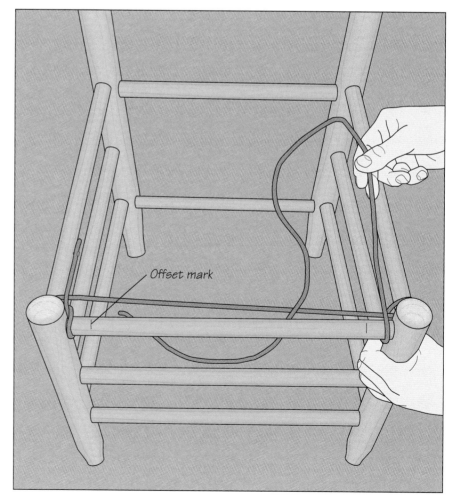

Offset mark

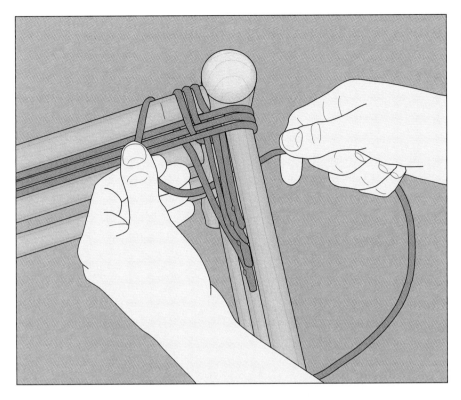

2 Squaring the seat frame
Fasten a length of rush alongside the first one, using the technique described in step 1. Loop it around the front and side rails and fasten it to the opposite rail. Continue adding lengths of rush *(left)* until you reach the offset marks you made on the front rail. Be sure to keep the rush as tight and straight as possible.

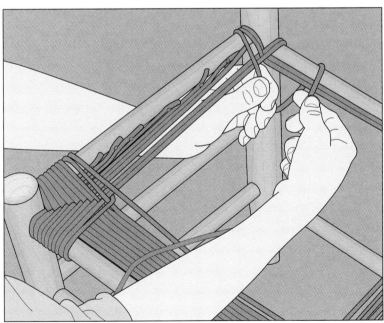

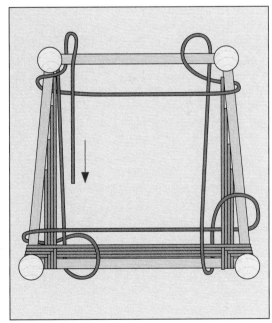

3 Weaving a complete circuit
Once you have squared the seat frame, you can begin rushing the seat all around the frame. Working with an approximately 20-foot length of rush, tack it to the side rail near the rear legs and loop it around all the rails *(above, left)*. Each complete circuit is known as a bout. Keep working around the chair using the same pattern *(above, right)*. When you get to the end of a length of rush, clamp it temporarily to the seat frame to keep it taut and attach it to a new piece using a figure-eight knot. Locate the knots on the underside of the seat so that they will not be visible.

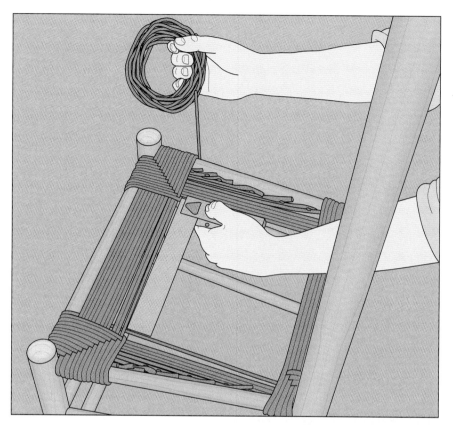

4 Checking the weave for square
Once every third or fourth circuit, check whether the sides of the seat are perpendicular to each other. Holding the length of rush in a coil with one hand, butt a try square in one corner of the seat *(left)*. The handle and blade of the square should rest flush against the rushing. If not, use a flat-tip screwdriver to straighten the side that is out-of-square, pushing the last circuit you installed against adjacent ones. Repeat at the remaining corners of the seat.

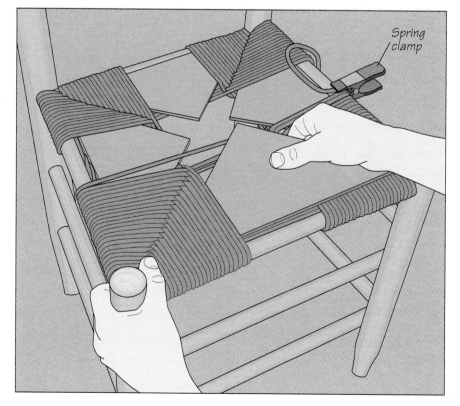

Spring clamp

5 Stuffing the seat
Once the rushing is about two-thirds done, it is time to stuff the seat. (The stuffing provides extra padding). To prevent the rush from slackening, use a spring clamp to secure the loose length you are installing to a seat rail. Use cardboard for the padding, cutting one triangular piece for each each side of the seat so that the triangle's long side is slightly shorter than the seat rail. Slip the padding under the rushing *(right)*, then trim the tips if they overlap in the center. Continue the normal circuit as before until the two side rails are covered.

6 Completing the bridge

On a seat that is deeper than it is wide, as in the chair shown here, the rushing being installed on the side rails will meet in the middle of the seat before the rush on the front and back rails. Once this occurs, use a technique known as bridging to fill the gap. Loop the rushing on the front and back rails with a figure-eight pattern weave, passing the rush over the back rail, down through the center, under the seat, and up around the front rail. Then bring the rush over the seat from the front rail and back down through the center *(right)*. Pass the rush under the seat, come up around the back rail again, and repeat.

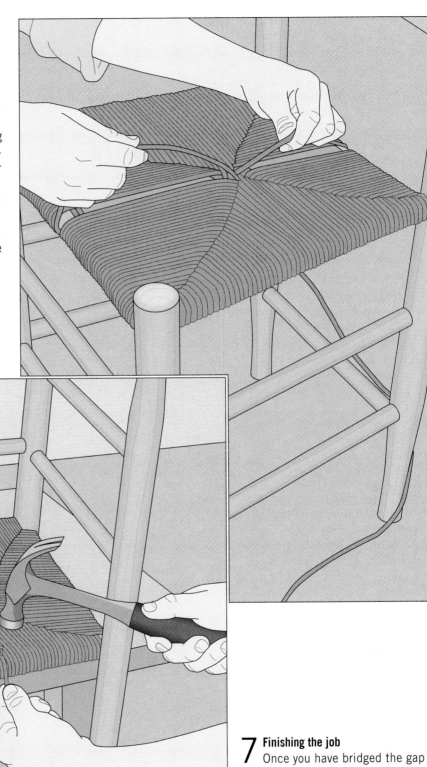

7 Finishing the job

Once you have bridged the gap between the front and back rails, set the chair upside down on a work table and tack the last strand of rush to the underside of the back seat rail *(left)*.

LEGS AND STRETCHERS

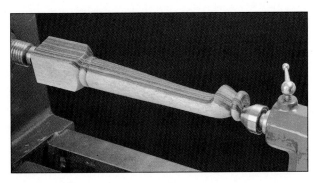

L egs and stretchers are a chair's foundation. It would be challenging enough if chairs were only sat upon; but they are often used as makeshift stepladders, or tilted back with the user's weight shifted onto the rear legs alone. It is the legs and stretchers that must withstand these and other abuses. Although the focus in this chapter is on the design and style of legs and stretchers, do not overlook the necessary joinery.

A footed leg can be fashioned on the lathe with a method known as off-center turning. The blank is first mounted true between centers and the pommel and basic cylinder are shaped. Then, the stock is remounted with the foot-end off-center to shape the lower end of the leg. Finally, the blank is remounted true to finish the bead on the foot.

The type and quality of joinery that fixes the legs and stretchers in place is key to ensuring a chair's longevity. In frame chairs, blind and angled mortise-and-tenons are the joints of choice, as described on page 25. Slab-and-stick chairs rely on round mortise-and-tenons, reinforced by wedges, to attach the legs to the seat *(page 52)*. Stretchers are crucial in stick chairs, particularly if you are using green wood, for maintaining the tension in the leg joints as the wood dries and shrinks. Refer to the appropriate sections of the Frame Chair and Slab-and-Stick Chair chapters once you are ready to join your legs to the chair.

This chapter will show you how to make a variety of sturdy chair legs, including perennial favorites such as the cabriole leg *(page 98)*, tapered leg *(page 101)*, and turned leg *(page 102)*. Three types of stretchers are also highlighted: turned *(page 103)*, cross *(page 106)*, and square *(page 107)*.

As you are making legs, remember that you must also take comfort and style into account. As explained in the treatment of chair design on page 16, the height of a chair leg, from floor to seat, is typically 17½ inches. But while this dimension may suit someone of average height and build, it is obviously not ideal for every individual. Keep in mind that chair users should be able to rest the soles of their feet on the floor when comfortably seated.

The leg style you choose for a chair should also be suited to the chair's eventual function and setting. A cabriole leg, for example, is an ideal choice for a side chair in a formal dining room, but its distinctive curves and traditional shape would be out of place on a bar stool or a baby high chair.

The sweeping curves of a cabriole leg are cut on a band saw. Since the shape of the leg must be outlined on two adjacent sides of the blank, short bridges of solid wood are left in the kerfs when the cuts are made on the first side. This way, the outline on the adjacent face will not be lost. Once the second side is cut, the bridges are severed.

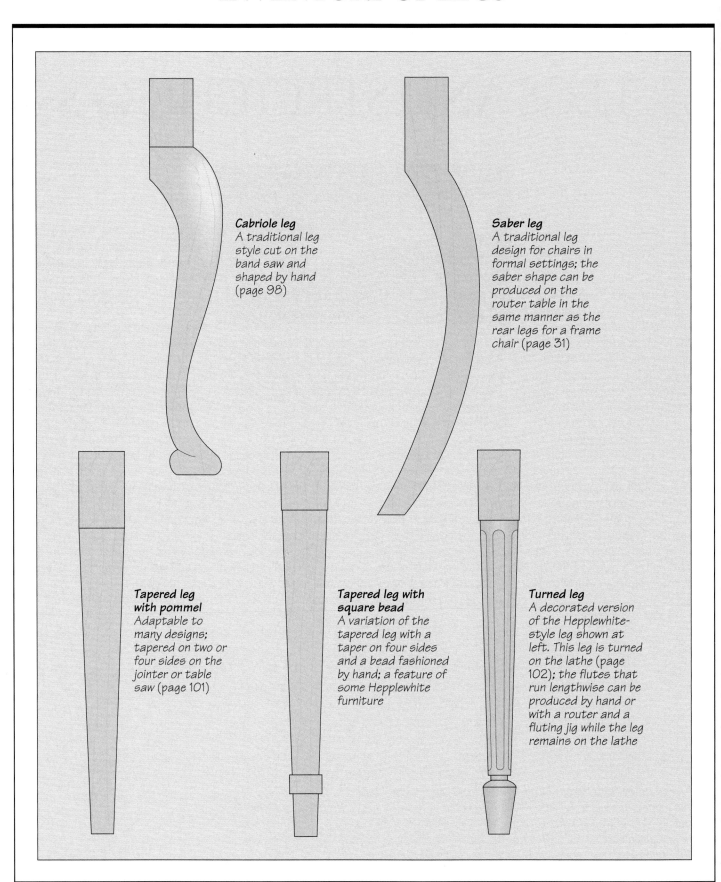

Cabriole leg
A traditional leg style cut on the band saw and shaped by hand (page 98)

Saber leg
A traditional leg design for chairs in formal settings; the saber shape can be produced on the router table in the same manner as the rear legs for a frame chair (page 31)

Tapered leg with pommel
Adaptable to many designs; tapered on two or four sides on the jointer or table saw (page 101)

Tapered leg with square bead
A variation of the tapered leg with a taper on four sides and a bead fashioned by hand; a feature of some Hepplewhite furniture

Turned leg
A decorated version of the Hepplewhite-style leg shown at left. This leg is turned on the lathe (page 102); the flutes that run lengthwise can be produced by hand or with a router and a fluting jig while the leg remains on the lathe

INVENTORY OF STRETCHERS

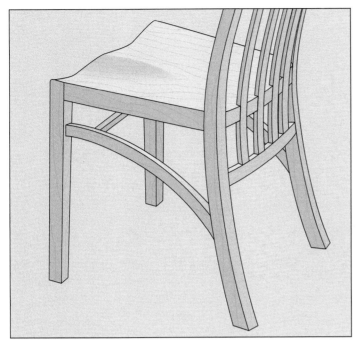

Curved stretchers
An elegant feature of a frame chair, this style of stretcher can be fashioned from bent-laminated stock or cut on a band saw; attached to the legs with dowels

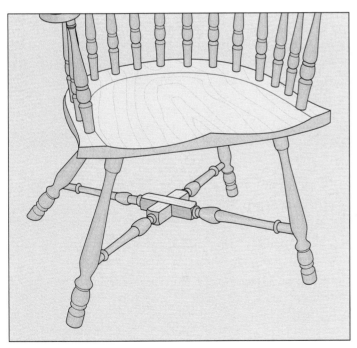

Cross stretchers
An attractive style for slab-and-stick chairs, but challenging to design and make; the stretchers meet with a lap joint at the center. They are cut on a table saw (page 106) and joined to the legs with round mortise-and-tenons

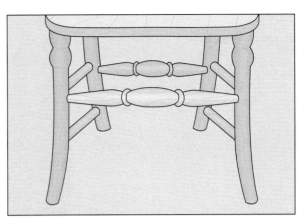

Turned stretchers
Ideally suited to slab-and-stick chairs with turned legs; produced on a lathe and joined to the legs with round mortise-and-tenons (page 103)

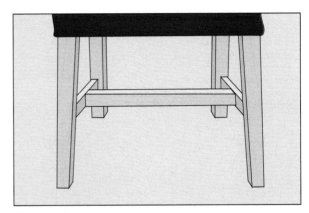

Square stretchers
A simpler variation of the cross stretcher well suited to frame chairs (page 107); stabilizes the legs

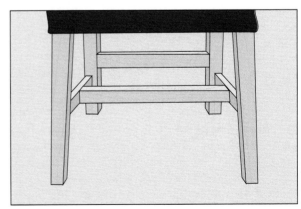

H stretcher with rear-leg stretcher
A variation of square stretchers that adds a stretcher between the rear legs and the square stretchers of a frame chair; provides strength while serving as a stylistic embellishment

LEGS

Three different leg styles; (from left to right) a tapered leg, with two adjacent sides sawn on a table saw; a cabriole leg cut on a band saw and shaped with a spokeshave; and a turned leg fashioned on a lathe.

CABRIOLE LEG

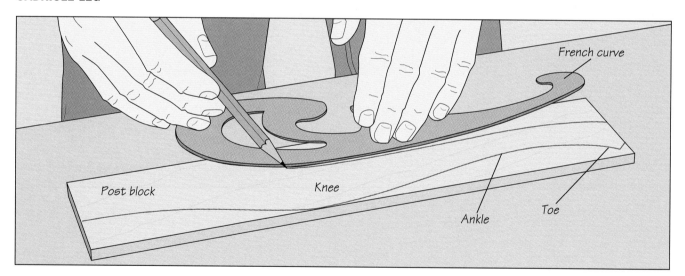

French curve

Post block   Knee   Ankle   Toe

1 Designing the leg

For a template, cut a piece of plywood or hardboard to the same length and width as your leg blanks. To draw the leg, start by outlining the post block. Make its length equal to the width of the rail that will be attached to the leg; the width should be adequate to accept the tenon of the rail (one-half to two-thirds the width of the stock is typical). Next, sketch the toe; for a leg of the proportions shown it should be about ¾ to 1 inch from the bottom of the leg. Then, using a french curve, draw the front of the leg from the toe to the ankle; at its nar-

rowest point, the thickness of the ankle should be about two-fifths the stock width. Move on to the knee, sketching a gentle curve from the post block to the front edge of the template 2 to 3 inches below the block. Then join the knee to the ankle with a relatively straight line. Complete the outline at the back of the leg, connecting the bottom of the leg with the back of the ankle. Then sketch a curve from the ankle to the bottom of the post block *(above)*. Experiment with the outline until you have a satisfactory design.

2 Transferring the design to the leg blank
Cut out your template on a band saw and sand the edges up to the marked outline. Hold the template flat on one inside face of the leg blank, making sure that the ends of the template and the blank are aligned and that the back of the post block is flush with the inside edge of the block of wood. Trace along the edges of the template to outline the leg. Turn the block and repeat the procedure on the other inside face *(right)*. At this point, some woodworkers prefer to make preparations for the joinery before cutting the leg. (It is easier to clamp and cut a mortise in a rectangular leg blank, for example, than to carry out the same procedures on a leg with pronounced contours.) Other woodworkers cut the leg first and then do the joinery.

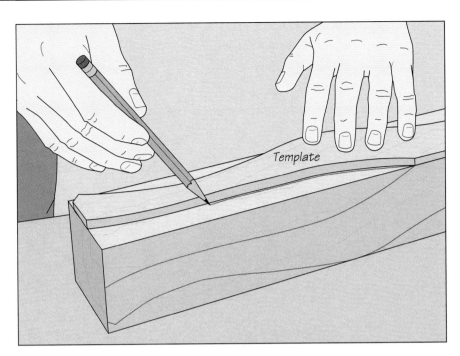

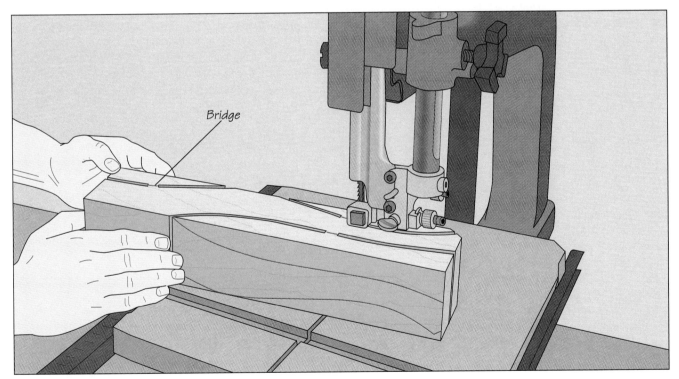

3 Making the cuts on one face of the leg
Set the leg blank on your band saw table with one of the marked outlines facing up and the bottom of the leg pointing away from you. Aligning the saw blade just to the waste side of the marked line for the back of the leg, feed the stock into the blade. Turn off the saw about halfway through the cut and remove the workpiece. Then cut along the same line from the opposite end. To avoid detaching the waste piece from the blank and losing the marked outline on the adjacent face, stop the cut about ½ inch from the first kerf, leaving a short bridge between the two cuts. Turn off the saw, retract the workpiece, then cut along the line for the front of the leg *(above)*.

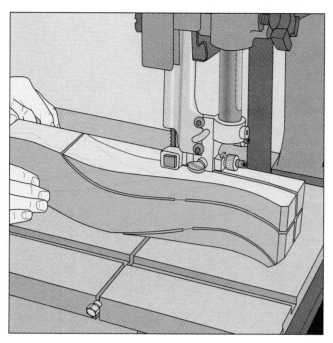

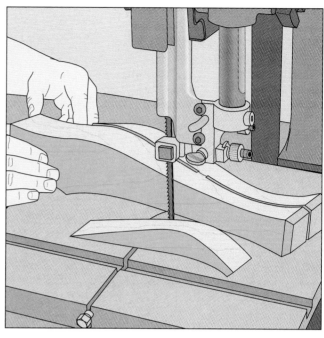

4 Making the cuts on the adjacent face
Turn the blank so that the marked outline on its adjacent side is facing up. Cut along the marked lines, begining at the foot *(above)*. This time, complete the cuts, letting the waste pieces fall away.

5 Cutting the bridges
Rotate the blank so that the first face you cut faces up. With the saw off, slide the blank forward to feed the blade into the kerf at the back of the leg. Turn on the saw and cut through the bridge to release the waste piece *(above)*. Then cut through the bridge between kerfs at the back of the leg.

6 Shaping and smoothing the leg
To finish shaping a cabriole leg and to remove any blemishes left by the band saw blade, smooth its surfaces with a spokeshave, followed by a rasp and sandpaper. Secure the leg in a bar clamp and fix the clamp to a work surface with a handscrew and C clamp as shown. Holding a spokeshave with both hands at the top of a curved edge of the leg, pull the tool slowly toward you, cutting a thin shaving and following the grain *(right)*. Repeat until the surface is smooth. Turn the leg in the bar clamp to clean up the other edges. Use the rasp to smooth an area that the spokeshave cannot reach. The tool works best when pushed diagonally across the grain. Finish the job with sandpaper, using progressively finer-grit papers until the surface is smooth.

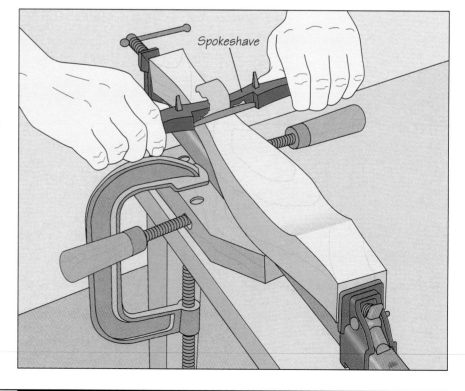

Spokeshave

TAPERED LEGS

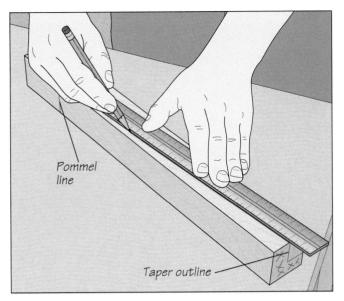

Pommel
line

Taper outline

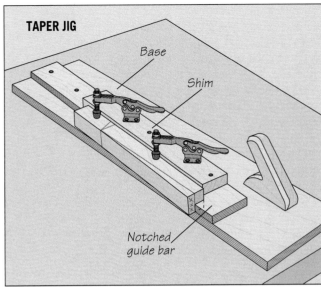

TAPER JIG

Base

Shim

Notched
guide bar

1 Making a taper jig

Mark a line all around the leg blank near the top end to define the square section, or pommel, to which the seat rails will be joined. Then outline the taper on the bottom end of the blank so that the bottom of the leg will be about ⅞ inch square. Use Xs to define the waste section. Next, mark the taper on two adjacent sides of the blank. Using a rule and a pencil, start each taper at the pommel line and end it at the taper outline on the bottom of the leg *(above, left)*. To cut the taper on your table saw, use a shop-made jig. Cut the jig base from

¾-inch plywood, making it longer and wider than the blanks. Set a blank on the base, aligning one taper line with the edge of the base. Hold the workpiece securely and position the plywood guide bar against it, fitting the end of the blank snugly into the notch. Screw the guide bar to the base, then fasten two toggle clamps to a solid wood shim. Screw the shim to the guide bar and press the toggle clamps down to secure the blank to the jig. Finally, fashion a handle and fasten it to the base *(above, right)*.

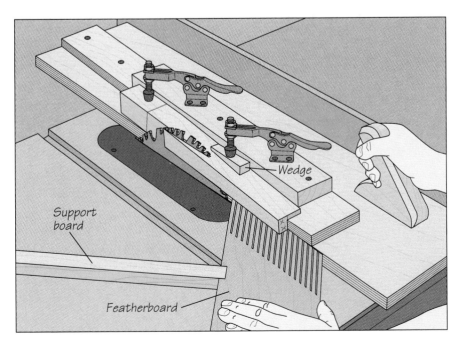

Support
board

Wedge

Featherboard

2 Tapering the leg

Butt the edge of the jig base with the blank against the blade and position the rip fence flush against the other side of the base. To support the blank during the cut, clamp a featherboard to the saw table, and brace it with a support board. To cut the first taper, slide the jig and workpiece across the table, making sure neither hand is in line with the blade. Then, release the toggle clamps, turn the blank to the adjacent side and reclamp it, this time using a wedge between the clamp and the tapered part of the leg. Feed the jig forward to taper the second side *(left)*. **(Caution: Blade guard removed for clarity.)**

TURNED LEGS

1 Defining the pommel
Mark a line all around the leg blank near the top end to define the pommel. Mount the blank between centers on your lathe and use a skew chisel to turn a rounded V-groove on the workpiece, starting about ½ inch below the pommel line. The groove will separate the square pommel from the cylindrical portion of the leg. Deepen the groove until it runs completely around the workpiece, then widen it by cutting with the long point of the chisel pointed forward. Rotate the handle from side to side so the bevel rubs against the sides of the groove *(right)*. Stop when you reach the pommel line.

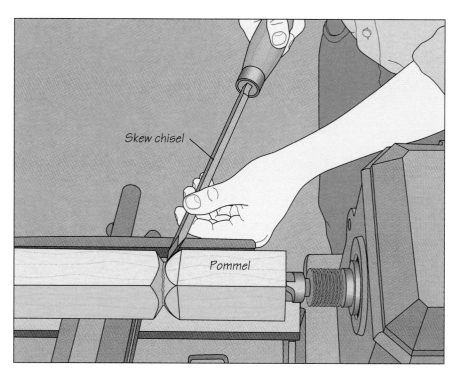

Skew chisel

Pommel

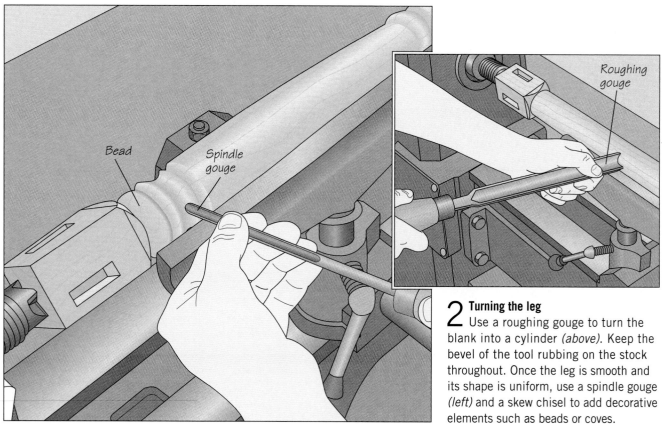

Bead

Spindle gouge

Roughing gouge

2 Turning the leg
Use a roughing gouge to turn the blank into a cylinder *(above)*. Keep the bevel of the tool rubbing on the stock throughout. Once the leg is smooth and its shape is uniform, use a spindle gouge *(left)* and a skew chisel to add decorative elements such as beads or coves.

STRETCHERS

Turned stretchers span the gap between the legs of the rocking chair shown at left. Apart from enhancing the appearance of a chair, stretchers provide structural support and can occasionally be designed to serve as footrests. Stretchers are usually made in the same way as the legs; in the example shown, the legs and stretchers are all turned. It is best to stagger the height of the stretchers; this way, the mortises in the legs will be at different locations and will not weaken the legs.

TURNED STRETCHERS

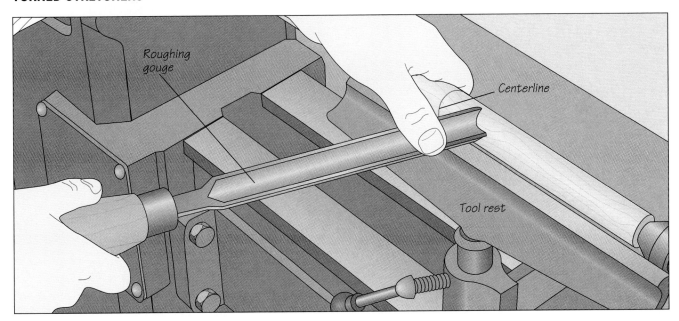

1 Turning the stretcher
Cut your stretcher blanks a little longer than their final dimension, mount a blank between centers on your lathe, and position the tool rest as close to the stock as possible without touching it. Use a roughing gouge to turn the blank to a cylinder, then turn off the lathe and mark the center of the blank with a pencil. Turn on the lathe and use the gouge to taper the stretcher from the centerline toward the ends. Support the tapered section with your free hand to prevent chatter *(above)*. Once you are satisfied with the shape of the stretcher, dry-assemble the legs and measure the gap between them at the height of the stretcher. Transfer your measurement to the blank, remembering that you must add a tenon at each end of the stretcher *(step 2)*.

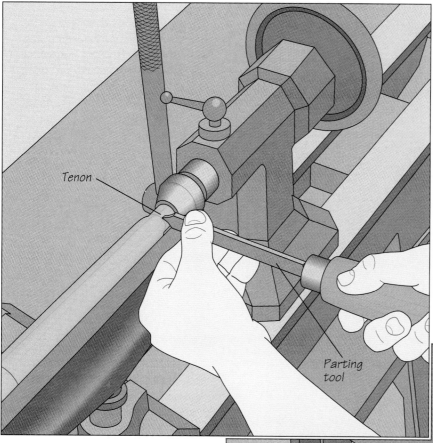

2 Turning the tenons
Use a parting tool to turn a tenon at each end of the stretcher *(left)*. To ensure a snug fit, make the diameter of the tenon equal to that of the bit you will use to bore the mortise. The length of the tenons should equal about one-half the leg thickness. If the tenons are too long, trim their ends.

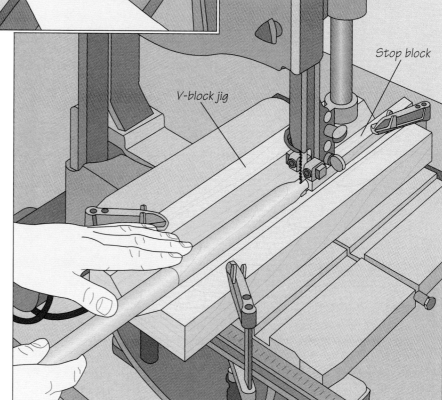

3 Kerfing the stretchers for wedges
Cut a V-shaped wedge out of a wood block, creating a jig that will hold the turned stretchers steady as you kerf the tenons. Cut a kerf about halfway along the bottom of the V, then place the stretcher in the jig and clamp the jig to your band saw table so the middle of the tenon is aligned with the blade. Holding the stretcher flat in the jig and positioning it so the kerf will be perpendicular to the grain of the leg, feed the stretcher into the blade. Stop the cut about ¼ inch from the tenon shoulder. Leave the stretcher in place, butt a stop block against the kerfed end, and clamp it to the jig. Kerf the remaining stretchers the same way *(right)*, stopping when the stock contacts the stop block.

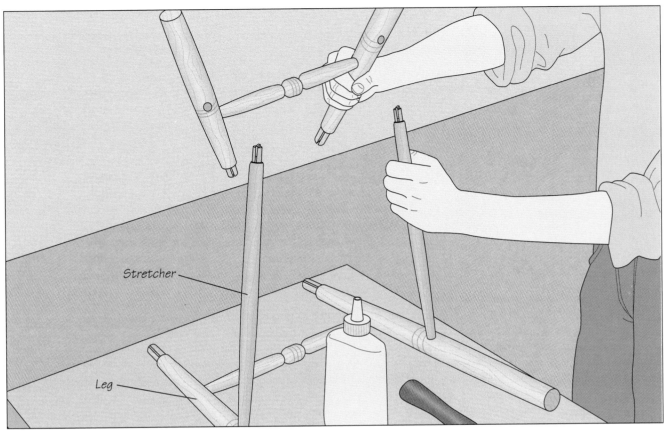

Stretcher

Leg

4 Assembling the legs and stretchers
Turned legs and stretchers for a stick chair are glued up at the same time. Bore the holes in the legs for the stretchers *(page 57)*, spread some glue on the tenon wedges, and insert them in their kerfs. Also apply adhesive to the tenons and in the mortises. Work on a flat surface to fit the legs and stretchers together *(above)*, using a dead-blow hammer to fully seat the tenons in the mortises.

SHOP TIP

Boring mortises for stretcher tenons on the drill press
The simple setup shown at right will help you adjust the angle of your drill press table to bore the holes for stretchers in the legs of a stick chair. Dry-fit the legs in the seat and clamp a board to two adjoining legs, positioning the board at the height where you will locate the stretchers. Then adjust a sliding bevel so the handle rests flush on the board and the blade is butted against one of the legs. Use the setting of the bevel to set the angle of your drill press table. Repeat for the remaining stretchers.

CROSS STRETCHERS

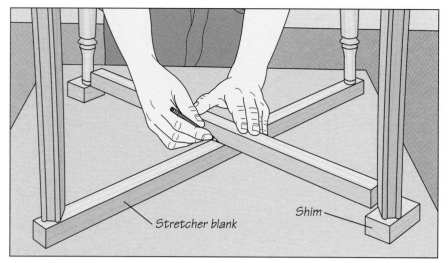

Stretcher blank

Shim

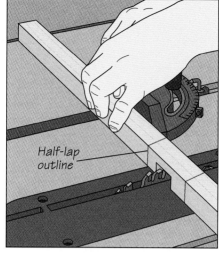

Half-lap outline

1 Sawing half-laps in the stretchers
Dry-assemble the chair and cut two stretcher blanks, making one slightly longer than the distance between diagonally opposite legs. Working on a flat surface, set the chair on the longer blank and place shims of the same thickness under the other legs. Then position the second blank between the shimmed legs and use a pencil to outline the area of overlap on both blanks *(above, left)*. Adjust a sliding bevel to the angle of the marks on the stretchers, then transfer the angle to your table saw's miter gauge. To saw the half-laps, set the cutting height to one-half the stretcher stock thickness. Hold one stretcher flush against the miter gauge with the middle of the half-lap outline aligned with the blade and butt the rip fence against the stock. Use the gauge to feed the stretcher into the blade, then turn the workpiece end-for-end, shift the fence toward the blade by the thickness of the saw kerf, and repeat the cut. Continue *(above, right)* until you cut to the marked lines. Repeat for the other stretcher. **(Caution: Blade guard removed for clarity.)**

2 Turning the stretchers
Outline a square section at the middle of both stretchers, locating the marks at least 1 inch beyond the shoulders of the half-laps. Then mount one of the stretchers between centers on your lathe. Start by using a skew chisel to define the square section *(page 102)* and a roughing gouge to turn the remaining portion into a cylinder. Repeat for the other stretcher. Once both stretchers are turned, place them under the chair legs as you did in step 1, this time with the pieces joined at the half-laps. Use a try square and a pencil to mark the points where the stretchers will enter the legs *(right)*, then finish turning the stretchers, adding tenons and kerfing them for wedges. Secure the stretchers in place *(page 105)*.

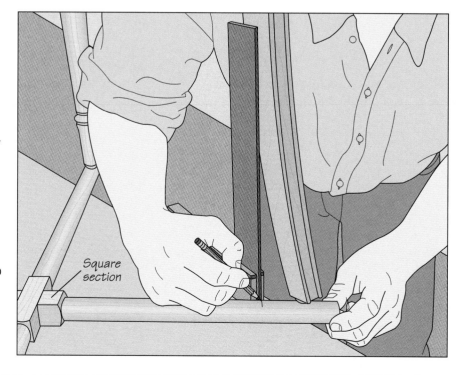

Square section

SQUARE STRETCHERS

1 Determining the angle between the front and rear legs

Because the front and rear legs of a frame chair are typically set at an angle to one another, and the surfaces of the legs themselves may be tapered or curved, you need to make a compound cut at the ends of the stretchers. This will ensure that the stretchers fit flush against the legs. To measure the angle between the front and rear legs, set your seat template *(page 26)* on a work surface and mark a line from the middle of one front leg to the middle of the rear leg directly opposite. Adjust a sliding bevel to the angle between the line and the front seat rail *(right)*.

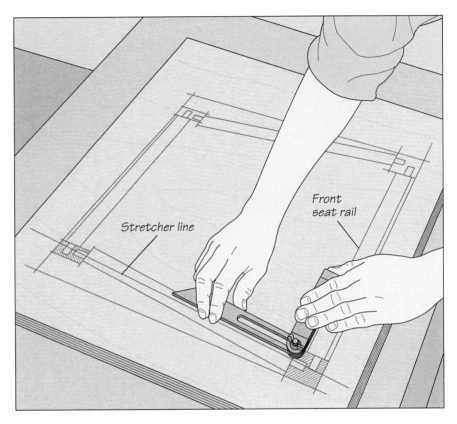

Stretcher line

Front seat rail

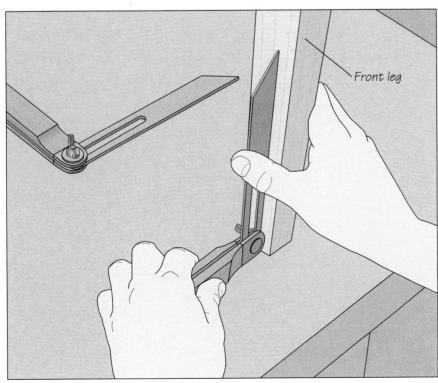

Front leg

2 Measuring the angle of the front leg surface

Dry-assemble the chair, set it on a work surface, and use a second sliding bevel to measure the angle between the table and the inside face of the front leg *(left)*.

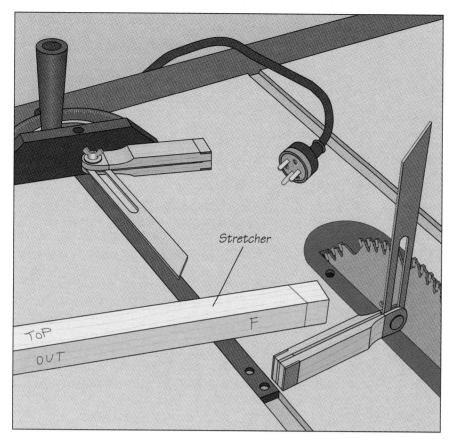

3 Setting up the table saw and cutting the stretchers

Transfer the angle from the sliding bevel you used in step 1 to your table saw's miter gauge and to the outside face of the stretcher blanks at the front-leg end. Use the sliding bevel from step 2 to adjust the table saw blade angle. Also transfer the angle to the top edge of the stretcher at the front-leg end *(left)*. Cut the front-leg end of both stretchers, using the miter gauge to feed the stock. Then repeat steps 1 and 2 to set up the saw for the back-leg ends of the stretchers and cut the stock to length.

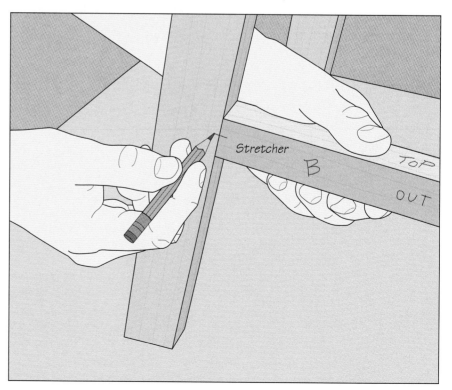

4 Marking the dowel joints between the legs and stretchers

Position one of the strechers between the front and rear legs and mark a line from the middle of the stretcher onto each leg *(right)*. Repeat for the other stretcher, then extend the lines on the legs to their inside edges.

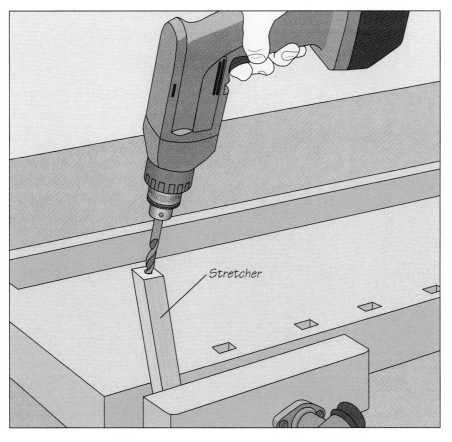

Stretcher

5 Drilling the dowel holes
Fit an electric drill with a bit the same diameter as the dowels you will use to join the stretchers to the legs. Bore a hole into each leg. The dowel holes should be slightly more than one-half as deep as the length of the dowels. To prepare the stretchers for the dowels, secure one of them end up in a bench vise with the cut end perfectly horizontal. Then, holding the drill perpendicular to the end of the stock, bore a hole of the proper depth into the stretcher *(left)*. Repeat at the other end of the stretcher and at both ends of the second stretcher.

6 Installing the stretchers
Dab glue in the dowel holes and insert the dowels into the stretchers. Fit the stretchers between the legs as you are gluing up the chair *(page 49)*, then clamp the assembly *(below)*, aligning the bar with the stretchers and using wood pads to protect the legs. Taper the wood pads as necessary so they rest flat on the legs.

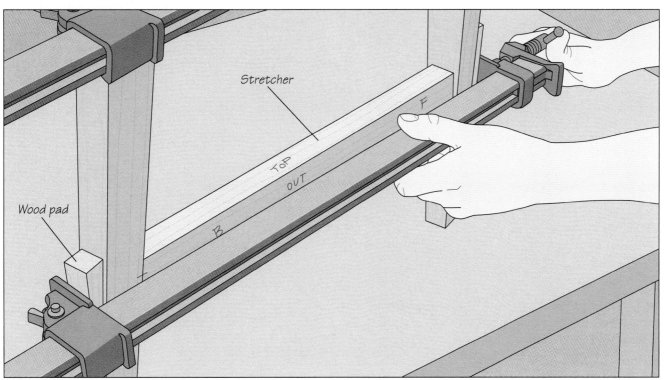

Stretcher

Wood pad

ARMS AND BACKS

A pair of chair arms is given a final sanding before being installed. Depending on the design of the chair, the arms can be left square or shaped with gentle curves, as in the graceful arms shown above.

Like other components of a chair, such as seats, rails, and legs, the arms and backs must be tailored to the shape and needs of the chair's user. Because they also contribute to both the support and the comfort provided by a chair, arms and backs are arguably the most demanding parts to design and build.

By definition, all chairs need backs; the arms are optional. Traditionally, dining chairs with arms were used only at the head and end of the table. These chairs often had higher backs, endowing the user with a more imposing presence. Since chairs with arms cannot be positioned close to a table or set close together, they are seldom used along the sides of tables. Hence, armless chairs became known as side chairs.

Woodworkers rely on several methods to attach arms to the frame of a chair. As shown on page 112, arms can be separate assemblies added to the chair after the frame is glued up, or made an integral part of the structure, as in the continuous arm of the popular Windsor chair.

This chapter will also explain two options for chair backs: the cane back and panel back. (Two versions of the slat back are shown in previous chapters. See page 43 for instructions on building a vertical slat back suitable for a frame chair, and page 61 for information on making a horizontal slat back for a slab-and-stick chair.) Both the cane back and the panel back employ a crest rail along the top and a back rail across the bottom to support the panel or the cane. In building chairs, the need for form to follow function quickly becomes evident. It is important to position the crest rail so it will not interfere with the user's head. As well, the back rail should feel comfortable against the lower back. The chapter on Frame Chairs *(page 22)* includes a detailed explanation of the joinery involved in installing backs.

The chair shown at left features extended post arms, giving the basic frame chair design a more formal appearance. To ensure that the arms do not crowd the chair's user, the seat is made a little wider than it might otherwise be. The back features slats similar to those made in the Frame Chair chapter (page 43).

ARM AND BACK STYLES

SEPARATE ARMS

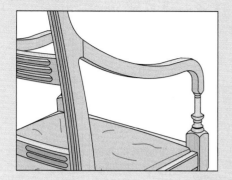

Attached to the front and rear legs with dowels or mortise-and-tenon joints (page 114)

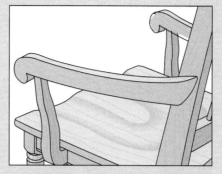

Attached to the rear legs with dowels or screws; fixed to seat rails with arm posts which are doweled or screwed (page 116)

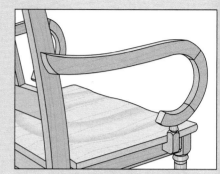

Fastened to rear legs with dowels or screws; attached to seat rail with a separate post

BACKS

Horizontal-slat back
Commonly used on slab-and-stick chairs (page 50)

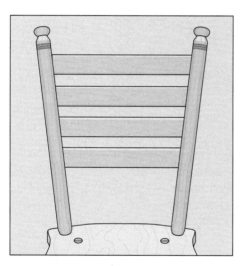

Mullion back with decorative crest rail
Turned mullions are mortised into underside of crest rail and top of seat, much like straight frame chair slats (page 43)

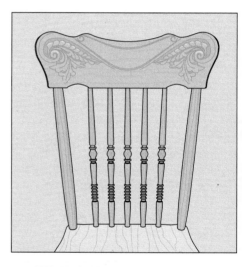

Cane back
Framed at top and bottom by crest and back rails, and on sides by vertical mullions (page 119)

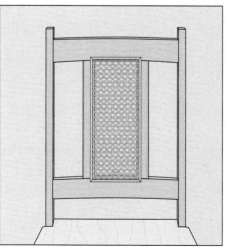

Upholstered back
Made like an upholstered seat (page 78) and installed in a rabbet cut around perimeter of back frame

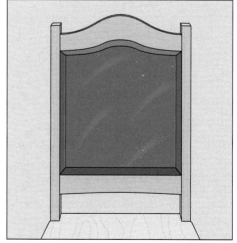

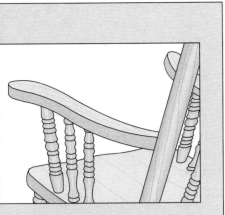

Attached to the rear legs with dowels or screws; fixed to seat with arm posts which are mortised into seat and underside of arms

CONTINUOUS ARM

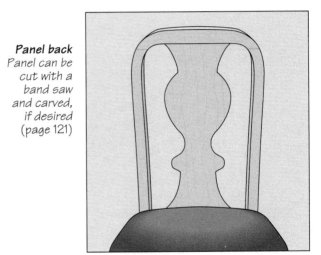

A Windsor chair continuous arm
Made of steam-bent solid stock or a bent lamination; secured to the chair with spindles that are mortised into the seat

Turned mullion back with shaped crest and back rails
Mullions are installed between the crest and back rails

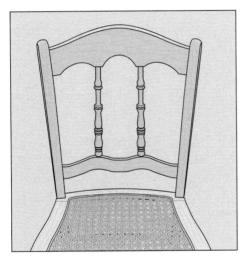

Panel back
Panel can be cut with a band saw and carved, if desired (page 121)

Vertical-slat back
A typical back for frame chairs (page 22)

Scrollwork panel-back
An embellished variation of the plain panel back shown above; the carved-rail backrest was typical of the American Chippendale style of the late 18th Century

ARMS

This section describes two methods for attaching arms to a frame chair. In the technique shown below and on page 115, the inside edges of the arms are flush with the outside edges of the seat. To keep the arms from crowding the chair user, the chair seat should be made wider than normal; 3 inches extra is about right. In addition, the front legs must be a few inches longer—high enough to extend above the seat and be joined to the bottom of the arms. If you are using this method, remember to prepare the front legs for the arms before assembling the chair.

In the second method *(left and page 116)*, the arms are supported by a separate post which is glued and screwed at the bottom to the side seat rails. The arms are then doweled to the post and screwed to the rear legs. This type of arm is built with the help of templates.

The separate arm on the frame chair shown at left was attached to the rear leg post with screws. The fasteners were counterbored and concealed with wood plugs.

EXTENDED-POST ARMS

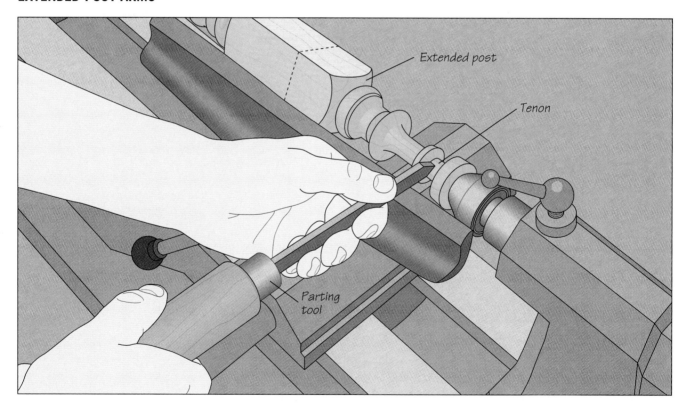

Extended post

Tenon

Parting tool

1 Preparing the legs for the arms
Turn the legs on a lathe as you would for a side chair *(page 102)*, but make the blanks several inches longer. The added length (the section to the right of the dotted lines in the illustration above) will enable the leg to extend above the seat and accept the bottom of the arm. Once you have turned the extended-post segment of the leg to a satisfactory shape, use a parting tool to produce a round tenon the top end of the leg *(above)*. The tenon will be glued into a hole in the bottom of the arm. When both legs are turned, you can glue up the chair.

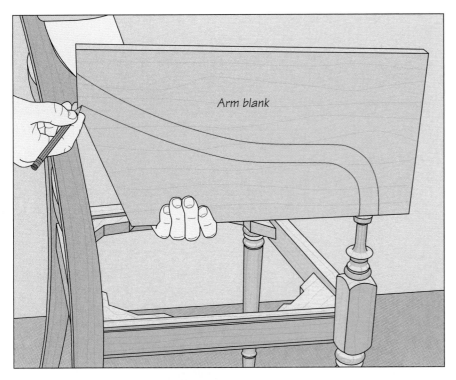

Arm blank

2 Making the arms

Prepare two pieces of solid stock as arm blanks. Then, holding one of the pieces in position against a rear leg and the front leg on the same side of the chair, mark the outline of the arm with a pencil *(left)*. Design the arm to be both comfortable and visually pleasing; its horizontal section normally should be 8 to 9 inches above the seat. Make sure the bottom of the outline is centered on the tenon you turned in step 1. Cut out the arm on your band saw and use it as a template to outline and cut the other arm. Drill a hole in the bottom end of each arm for the front leg tenon and another in the top end for a dowel joining it to the rear legs. Shape the arms to suit the design of the chair and sand their surfaces smooth. This type of arm can also be made as a bent lamination as you would to produce rockers for a rocking chair *(page 130)*.

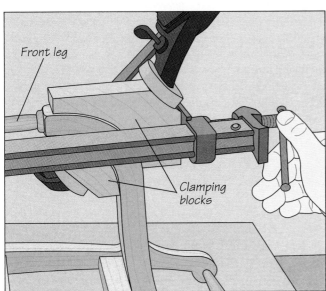

Front leg

Clamping blocks

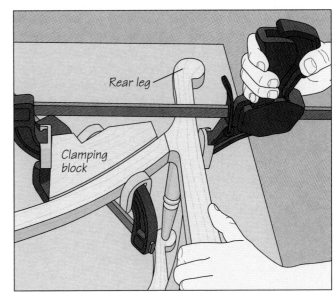

Rear leg

Clamping block

3 Installing the arms

Test-fit the arms on the chair. Their ends should lie flush on the legs; sand the ends to fit, if necessary. Remember to drill dowel holes in the rear legs. When the arms are ready to be glued up, cut clamping blocks that will enable you to apply pressure squarely on the arms. At each front leg, cut two blocks, each with a curved edge to follow the contours of the arm and a flat edge to accept the clamp jaw. Apply glue to the tenon on the front leg and the holes in the arm, insert the dowel into the rear leg, and fit the arm in place. Clamp the blocks to the arm, then install a bar clamp to secure the arm to the front leg, placing one jaw on the block and the other on the bottom of the leg. Tighten the clamp until the joint is snug *(above, left)*. At the rear leg, clamp a single block to the arm, then pull the joint snug with a second clamp, placing one jaw on the block and the other on the back edge of the rear leg *(above, right)*.

SEPARATE-POST ARMS

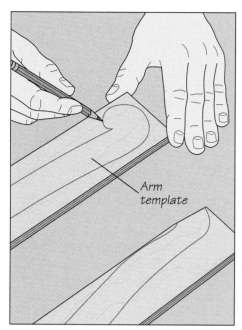

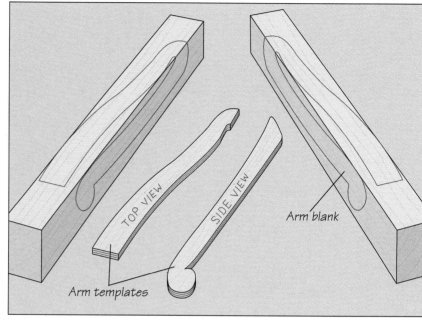

Arm template

TOP VIEW

SIDE VIEW

Arm blank

Arm templates

1 Making the arms

Because separate-post arms curve outward as well as downward, making them requires two templates: one representing the top view of the arm and the other showing the side view. Outline each view on a piece of ¼-inch plywood or hardboard the same length as the arms *(above, left)*. The shapes should suit the design of the chair, but make sure the inside back end of the arm is flat so that it can be fastened flush against the

outside face of the rear leg *(step 5)*. Once you have completed the outlines, label them and cut them out on your band saw. Then trace the outlines on adjacent faces of two arm blanks, making sure the back ends of the outlines are aligned at the same end of each blank. Also ensure that the outlines on the blanks are mirror-images of each other *(above, right)*. Band saw the arms as you would a cabriole leg *(page 99)*.

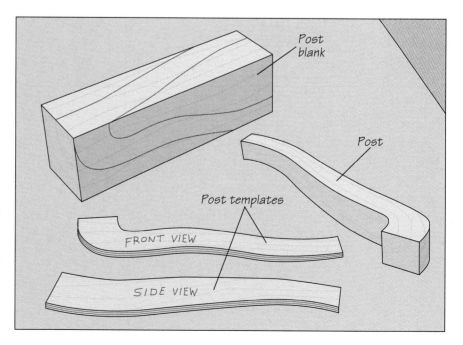

Post blank

Post

Post templates

FRONT VIEW

SIDE VIEW

2 Making the posts

Make the posts as you did the arms, producing two templates, transferring the outlines to two blanks and cutting them on the band saw *(right)*. Both ends of each post should be flat; the bottom is fastened flush against the outside face of the side seat rail *(step 3)* and the top is attached to the underside of the arm *(step 4)*. Sand the arms and posts smooth.

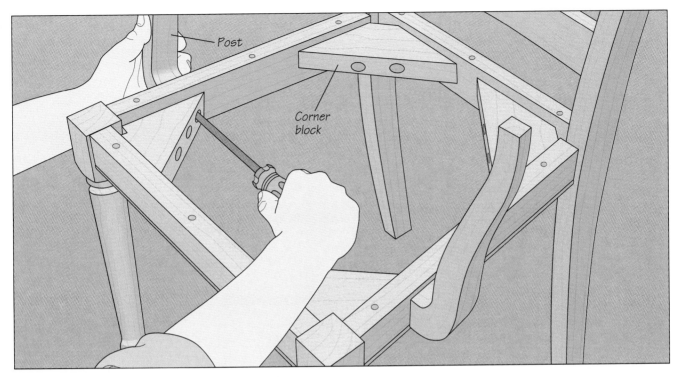

3 Attaching the posts to the side seat rails

To help you position the posts against the side seat rails, test-fit the arms and posts in place. Once you are satisfied with the placement of the pieces, mark the post location on the rail. In the example shown above, each post will be fastened to its rail with a countersunk screw 4 inches from the front end of the rail. Drill a clearance hole for the screw shank through the corner block and the rail. Enlarge the top of the hole with a larger bit to recess the screw head and use a smaller bit to bore a pilot hole into the bottom end of the post. Then, holding the post in place against the rail, screw it in place. Repeat with the other post *(above)*. Leave the screws a little slack for now so you can trim the posts or adjust their positions later, if necessary.

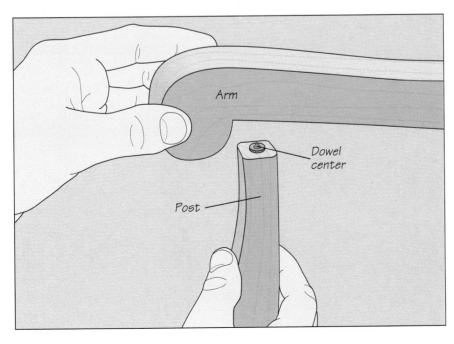

4 Preparing the arms and posts for dowels

Drill a hole into the center of the top end of each post slightly deeper than one-half the length of the dowels you will be using. Insert a matching dowel center into the hole, then position the arm against the rear leg, align the arm with the post, and press the arm against the center *(left)*. Its pointed end will punch an indentation into the underside of the arm, providing you with a starting point for drilling the dowel hole. Before moving the arm, outline its position on the rear leg so you can reposition it properly later. Drill the matching dowel hole in the arm to the same depth as that in the post.

5 Attaching the arms to the rear legs
Test-fit one arm on its rear leg and sand the end of the arm, if necessary, so it lies flat on the leg. Once you are satisfied with the fit, counterbore a clearance hole for a screw through the leg. Then, holding the arm in place against the leg, drive the screw until its tip scores the arm. Remove the arm, drill a pilot hole at the marked point, and fasten the arm to the leg *(above)*, leaving the screw a little slack so you can lower the arm onto the dowel in the post *(step 6)*. Repeat for the other arm.

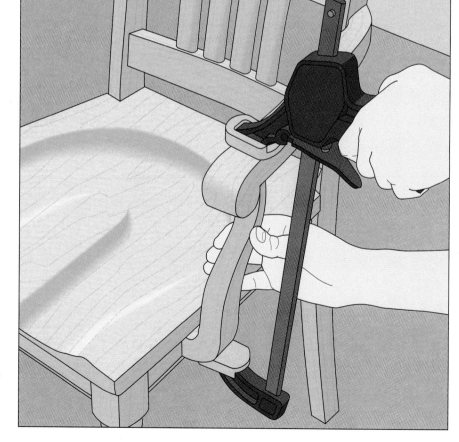

6 Gluing the arms to the posts
Dab a little glue into the dowel holes in the posts and arms, and insert a dowel into each post, tapping it down with a rubber mallet. Lower the arm onto the dowel and secure the joint with a clamp *(right)*. Finish tightening all the screws.

BACKS

C aned and panel backs are two popular and attractive options for frame chairs. To make a caned back *(below)*, all you need is some stock for the rails and mullions and a piece of prewoven cane. You can weave the back from individual strands of cane, following instructions starting on page 83. Cut tenons at the ends of the rails to fit into mortises in the rear legs and at the ends of the mullions to join with the rails. The cane fits into a groove cut into the rails and mullions.

The panel for a panel back is cut on a band saw *(page 122)*, then fitted into grooves cut into the edges of the back and crest rails. Glue is not used to fix the panel so it can move. The bottom edge of the crest rail is usually shaped to accept the curved top of the panel.

The caned back on the chair shown at right is framed by crest and back rails and a pair of vertical mullions. The prewoven cane is wedged into grooves cut into the rails and mullions and held in place by a wooden spline.

A CANED BACK

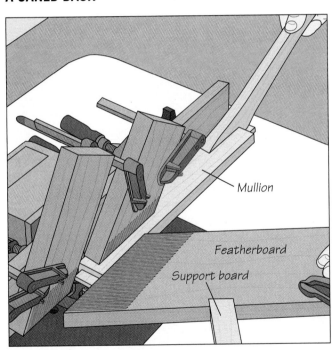

Mullion

Featherboard

Support board

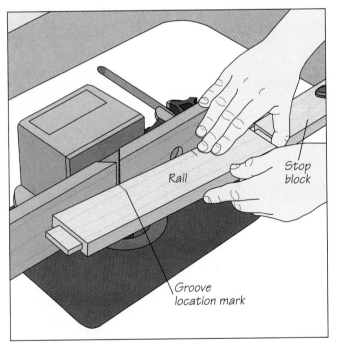

Rail

Stop block

Groove location mark

1 Preparing the rails and mullions
Cut the grooves in the rails and mullions on a router table. Use a straight bit with a diameter equal to the width of the spline you will use to secure the cane; adjust the cutting height to slightly more than the thickness of the spline. Start with the mullions, using three featherboards to support them during the cut: Clamp two to the fence, one on each side of the bit, and a third to the table, braced by a support board. Position the fence to cut the groove ¼ inch from the edge of the mullions, then feed the boards with a push stick *(above, left)*. Before routing the grooves in the rails, test-fit the rails and mullions together

and mark the location of the mullion grooves on the back face of the rails. Then remove the featherboards from the router table, align the groove mark on the leading end of the rail with the bit, and clamp a stop block to the table flush against the trailing end of the stock. Repeat the same process with the second groove mark to install a stop block that will limit the length of cut. Carefully lower the stock onto the bit, keeping the edge flush against the fence and the trailing end butted against the stop block *(above, right)*. Once the rail is flat on the table, feed it along the fence, lifting it clear once the stock touches the front stop block.

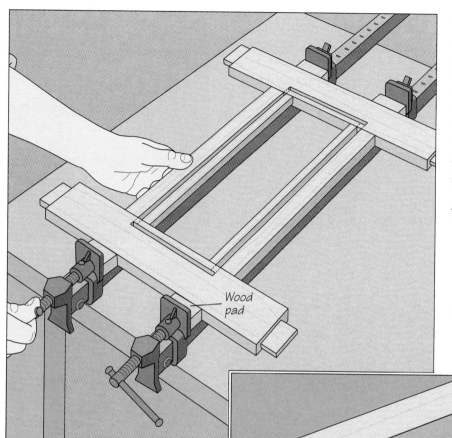

Wood
pad

2 Assembling the rails and mullions

Spread some glue on the tenons on the mullions and in the mortises in the rails, then fit the pieces together. Use two bar clamps to secure the joints, aligning the bars along the length of the mullions and protecting the rails with wood pads *(left)*. Once the glue has cured, use a chisel to complete the grooves between the rails and mullions. (The chisel cuts are represented by dotted lines in the illustration.) Then glue the caning frame to the chair, fitting the tenons on the rails into the rear legs (page 47).

Spline

Wedge

3 Fitting the cane in the chair back

While the glue is curing, soak a slightly oversized piece of cane in a bucket of warm water for at least two hours. The soaking will make the cane more pliable and easier to work. Many woodworkers will also finish the chair before installing the cane. Once you are ready, set the chair on its back on a work surface and position the cane over its opening. Use wedges at 3- to 4-inch intervals to press the cane into the groove in one of the mullions while pulling the cane taut on the opposite side *(right)*. Continue all around the frame.

4 Securing the cane

Cut the reed splines that will hold the cane to fit in the grooves, mitering both ends of each piece, then work on one side of the frame at a time to fix the cane in place permanently. Starting with one mullion, remove the wedges from its groove and, tapping a chisel with a wooden mallet, trim the excess cane flush with the outside edge of the channel. Then spread some glue on the underside of the spline and pound it in place with the mallet. Wipe away any glue squeeze out, then repeat the process with the opposite mullion *(right)* and the two rails.

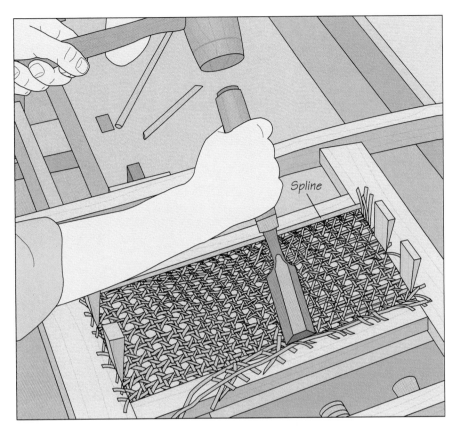

A PANEL BACK

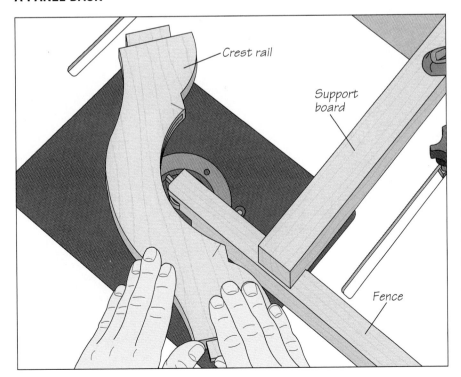

1 Preparing the rail

To make a panel back for a chair, start by routing grooves in the crest and back rails to accept the panel. Install a piloted three-wing slotting cutter in a router and mount the tool in a table; the cutter thickness should equal that of the panel. Adjust the cutting height by placing the stock face down on the table and aligning a cutter with the center of the edge. Fashion a fence for the stock on the infeed side of the table, cutting a notch at one end to cover the bit. Screw the fence to a support board and clamp the pieces to the table. Mark the start and end of the groove on the rails, then press the workpiece against the pilot bearing as you feed the stock into the bit against the direction of cutter rotation *(left)*.

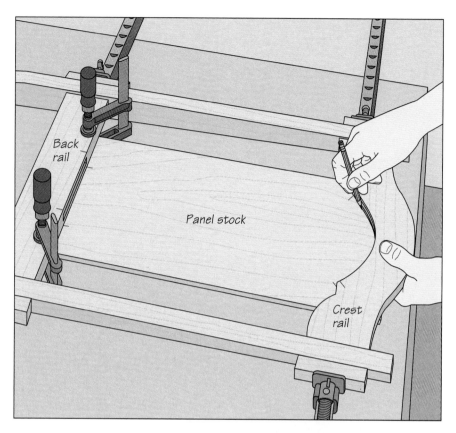

2 Outlining the top and bottom of the panel

To help you shape the panel and cut it to length, dry-assemble the rails and rear legs and clamp them together. Center the assembly atop the panel on a work surface, then clamp the panel to the back rail so the bottom of the panel extends under the rail by the depth of the groove, about ⅜ inch. Mark the start and end of the rail grooves at both the top and bottom of the panel. Then, holding the panel flush against the underside of the crest rail, trace the curve of the rail on the panel *(left)*. Remove the panel from the frame and mark a second line parallel to the first about ⅜ inch beyond it to allow for the portion of the panel that will extend into the groove.

3 Cutting the panel

Outline the sides of the panel, using any pattern that suits the design of the chair, but make sure the outlines begin and end at the groove marks at the top and bottom of the panel. To ensure that the two sides end up identical, outline just one side on a template. Then trace the pattern from the template to one side of the panel and turn the template over to outline the opposite side. Cut the panel on your band saw *(right)*, feeding the workpiece across the table and keeping your hands clear of the blade.

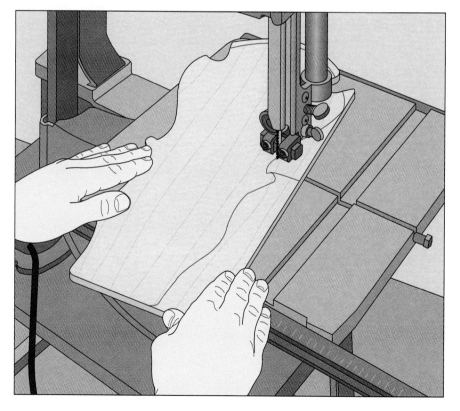

4 Test-fitting the panel

Take the panel frame apart and fit the panel into the back and crest rails *(right)*. Since the grooves cut by the router will be rounded at the ends, it may be necessary to trim the corners of the panel with a chisel or sandpaper to improve the fit.

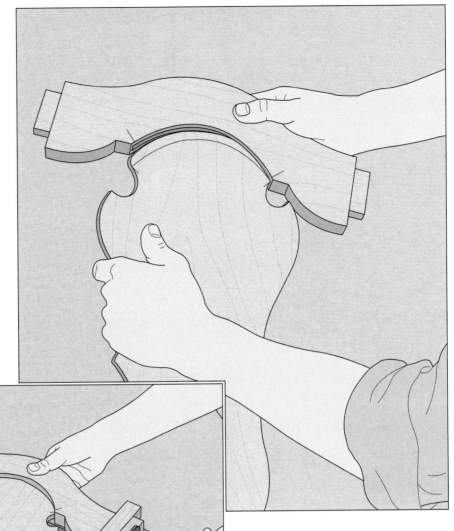

5 Gluing up the back

Spread some glue on the contacting surfaces of the rails and rear legs. Do not apply any adhesive in the panel grooves or the panel; the panel must be free to move as humidity changes cause the wood to swell or contract. Start assembling the back by fitting the back rail into the legs, then slip the panel into its groove in the back rail. Fit the crest rail onto the panel and into the rear legs. Close up the joints with two bar clamps *(left)*, aligning the bars with the rails and using wood blocks to protect the legs.

Clamping blocks

ROCKING CHAIRS

Built by renowned California furniture designer Sam Maloof, this rocking chair masterfully balances the elements of strength, comfort, and esthetics. The chair is built from fiddleback maple and features laminated rockers.

Evoking images of lazy summer evenings on the front porch or cozy winter afternoons indoors before a crackling fire, the rocking chair is a favorite place to relax for young and old alike. It is hard not to be seduced by a good rocking chair's insistent, swaying charms. Rare is the country cottage that is without one.

Descended from the rocking cradle, the rocking chair first appeared in America during the mid-18th Century. The earliest known model was a Windsor chair on curved slats. By 1840 Connecticut chair maker Lambert Hitchcock had adapted the design to include a stenciled crest rail and arms that followed the curve of the seat. This was the prototypical Boston Rocker that was widely imitated by many New England cabinetmakers.

For a time, the rocking chair proved more popular in the New World than the Old, but Viennese cabinetmaker Michael Thonet changed all that in 1860 with his bentwood rocker that quickly became the rage in Europe. Most rocking chairs built today are variations of these proven designs.

Despite the clean lines and balance a rocking chair must possess, you do not need an advanced course in geometry to make one. Armed with a few dimensions and angles *(page 127)*, some plywood for templates, and stock to experiment with, you can apply some basic principles to build a rocking chair just as easily as a frame or stick chair.

Like any chair, a rocking chair must support the weight of the person sitting in it. But because it also rocks back and forth, a rocker is subject to more stress than the average ladderback. The key to crafting a solid rocking chair lies in combining the right joinery with your design *(page 126)*; the chapter that follows shows one basic design and focuses on making the rockers and attaching them to the chair.

Once you have mastered these fundamental principles, you are free to experiment. But remember that a rocking chair must keep strength, comfort, and esthetics in balance. Each has its own requirements, and you should be willing to sacrifice a little of each to build a chair that is sturdy, pleasing to the eye, and comfortable.

Glued to the rockers, platforms are a way of fine-tuning the balance of a rocking chair before installing the rockers. In the photo at left, waste wood is removed with a rasp, smoothing the transition between the rockers and the legs.

ANATOMY OF A ROCKING CHAIR

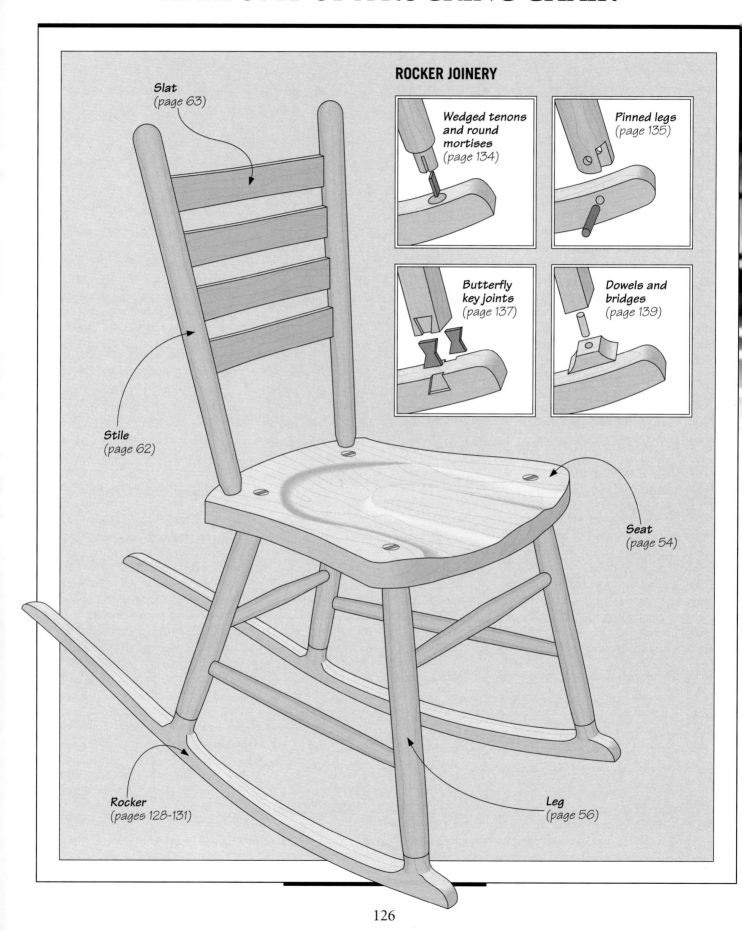

Slat
(page 63)

ROCKER JOINERY

Wedged tenons and round mortises
(page 134)

Pinned legs
(page 135)

Butterfly key joints
(page 137)

Dowels and bridges
(page 139)

Stile
(page 62)

Seat
(page 54)

Rocker
(pages 128-131)

Leg
(page 56)

ROCKER DESIGN

While the balance of a rocking chair can be fine-tuned at the assembly stage *(page 132)*, a few key principles and dimensions are worth noting before you begin. As shown in the illustration below, these include the height of the seat off the floor, the angle between the seat and the backrest, and the shape and arc of the rockers.

The height of the seat depends on the needs of the chair's user. Sitting comfortably on the seat, users should be able to rest their feet on the floor and rock the chair without effort. For most people, a seat height ranging between 12 and 16 inches will work well.

For a graceful-looking chair, design a 5° to 10° angle between the seat and the backrest. This will shift the weight and center of gravity toward the back of the chair. You can make the chair more comfortable for heavy-set users by trimming the back legs, which will increase the angle of the backreat.

The shape and arc of the rocker *(page 128)* are key factors that can ultimately make or break a rocking chair's design. A well-balanced rocking chair should come to rest about 2 inches in front of the rear legs, tilting the backrest 20° to 25° from the vertical. It should not pitch forward or backward when someone gets in or out of it, nor should it "walk" across the floor when it is rocked.

Finally, by experimenting with the curve of the rockers or the shape of their edges, or by splaying them slightly inward at the back, you can alter the way that a chair rocks.

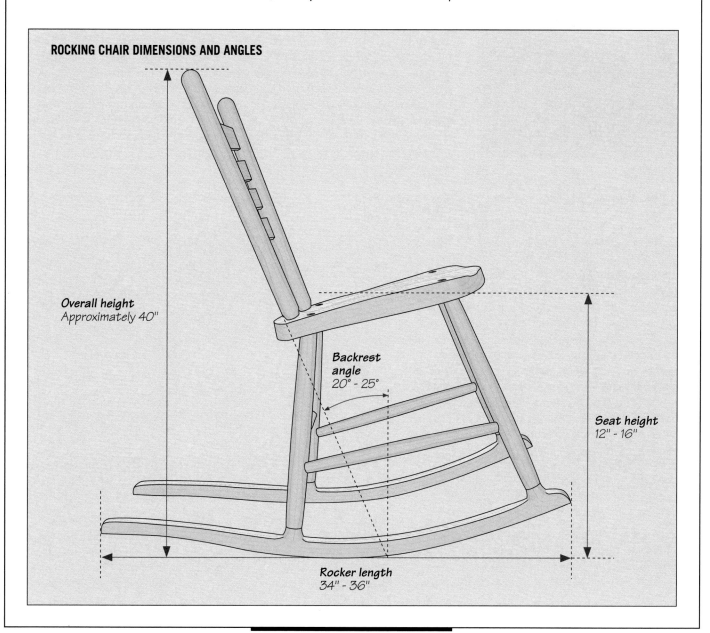

ROCKING CHAIR DIMENSIONS AND ANGLES

Overall height
Approximately 40"

Backrest angle
20° - 25°

Seat height
12" - 16"

Rocker length
34" - 36"

Determining the right shape for a rocking chair's rockers, also known as runners, is an exercise in experimentation and intuition. When designing a new chair, some chair makers try variations on a basic curve until they arrive at a design that is pleasing to the eye.

To ensure stability, however, the rockers must do more than look good. As a starting point, use a radius of 36 inches to 40 inches to draw the curve of the rocker. This curve is related to the height of the chair's seat off the floor and the height of the person sitting in the chair: The higher off the ground the seat is, and the taller the chair's user, the larger the arc of the rocker should be. Remember that the tighter the curve, the faster the chair will rock.

In addition to the rockers' primary curve, you can incorporate a reverse curve at the back end of the rocker, as shown in the chair on page 127. The reverse curve should be gentle, however; if the end of the rocker is not above the bottom of the rocker's primary curve, the chair will not rock properly.

Rockers can either be cut from a single piece of stock (below), or laminated from ⅛-inch-wide strips of resawn stock glued together in a bending form (page 130). Resawing on the table saw with a sharp, carbide-tipped blade will yield precise results without the need for sanding afterwards.

A laminated rocker is smoothed on an oscillating spindle sander. Laminated rockers, like the one shown at left, offer several advantages over rockers cut from solid wood. They can be made from narrower stock, which minimizes waste. They can also be made thinner since the strength of the glue bonding the strips together parallels the grain.

USING A TEMPLATE

1 Designing the bottom edge of the rockers
To make a template for the rockers, cut a piece of plywood or hardboard to the length of the rockers—in this case, about 34 inches. Then cut a thin strip of springy wood to the same length as the template. Using a C clamp and a stop block, secure the strip on edge to one end of the template. Then gently bend the strip into a curve that looks suitable for your rocker, securing the piece of wood in place with clamps and a stop block as shown. (You can using an existing rocking chair as a guide.) If you are including a reverse curve at the back end of the rockers, as shown at right, make sure the back end of the strip is at least 1 inch above the bottom of the curve. Clamping the strip firmly in place, run a pencil along it to define the rocker's bottom edge.

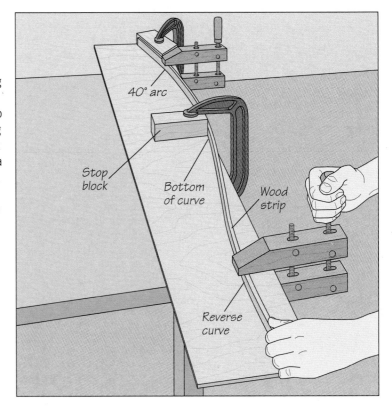

40° arc

Stop block

Bottom of curve

Wood strip

Reverse curve

2 Cutting the template

On your band saw, cut the template along the line you marked in step 1 and sand the cut edge smooth. To complete the outline of the rockers, mark a line that is parallel to the cut edge, spacing the line from the edge according to the desired height of the rockers. Round the outline at the front end and taper it slightly at the back. Bevel the back end of the outline by joining the line and the edge of the template with a straight line *(right)*. Cut out the template on the band saw.

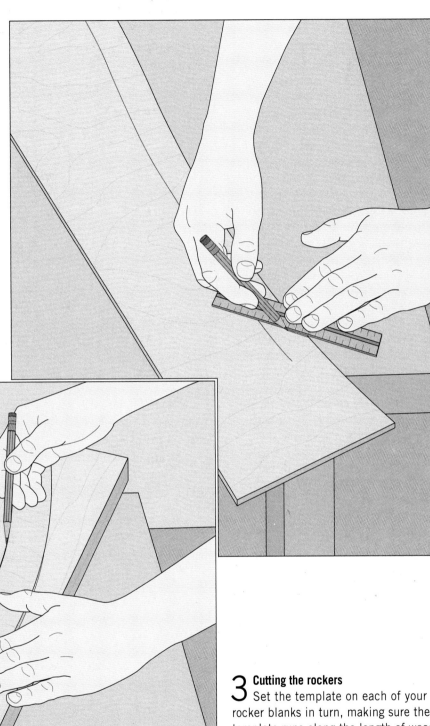

3 Cutting the rockers

Set the template on each of your rocker blanks in turn, making sure the template runs along the length of wood grain on the stock. Outline the template on the blank with a pencil *(left)*, then cut away most of the waste on the band saw. Shape the rockers to their final size on a router table as you would for the rear legs of a frame chair *(page 31)*.

BENDING LAMINATED STRIPS

1 Making the bending form
To bend the wood strips that will make up the rockers, build a bending form from two pieces of 1½-inch-thick stock *(right, top)*. The desired shape of the rocker's top and bottom edges is cut into the edges of the pieces of the form, then the strips are clamped in the form as they are glued together, bending the strips to the desired shape. Make the first piece of the form by marking the bottom edge of the rockers on it as you would if using a template *(page 128)*. Cut the piece along the curve and sand the cut edge. To make the second, or fixed, piece of the form, mark the same curve along it, then cut the strips—typically ⅛ inch thick—that will make up the rocker. Butt the strips face to face and measure their combined thickness; this will be the height of the rockers. Mark another line on the second piece, using your measurement to space the two lines *(right, bottom)*. Cut the fixed piece of the form along this line and sand the cut edge. Apply a thin coat of wax on the cut edges of both halves of the form to prevent the stock from sticking to them, then screw the fixed piece of the form to a base of ¾-inch plywood and mark the middle of the curve on it with a pencil.

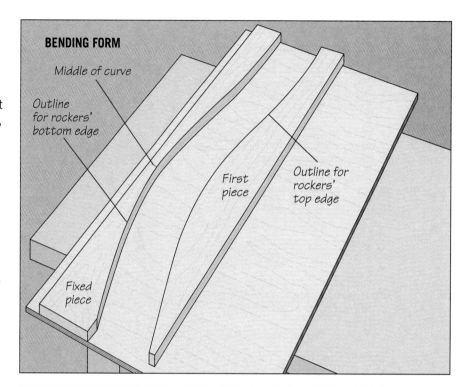

BENDING FORM

Middle of curve

Outline for rockers' bottom edge

First piece

Outline for rockers' top edge

Fixed piece

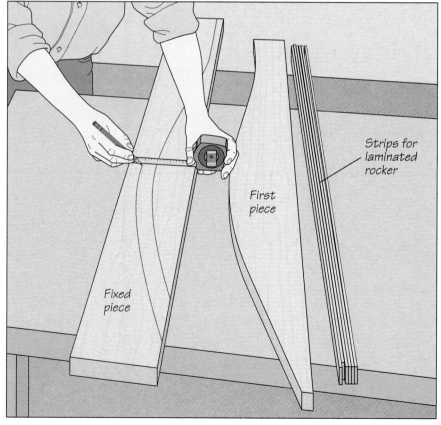

Strips for laminated rocker

First piece

Fixed piece

2 Gluing up and bending the rockers

Line the inside of the bending form with wax paper. Butt the strips for one rocker together and mark a line across their center. Spread glue on one side of each strip and butt them together again, lining up the center marks. Set the strips against the fixed half of the bending form, aligning the center marks on the form and the lamination. Butt the other half of the form against the strips and push it to bend the strips slightly. Install a bar clamp across the middle of the bend then, working from the middle toward the ends of the rocker, bend and secure the lamination with bar clamps, tightening each one in turn until there are no gaps along the rocker (right). Let the lamination cure for 8 to 10 hours, then repeat for the other rocker.

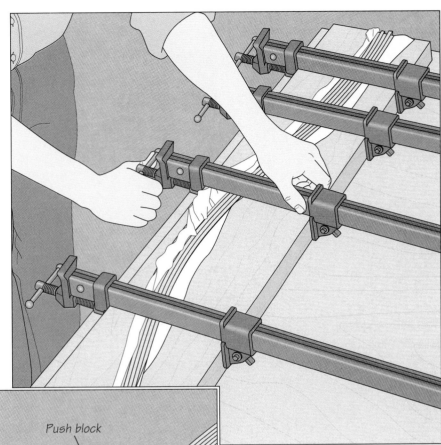

Push block

3 Jointing the rocker

Once the lamination is dry, remove it from the form, scrape away any excess glue, and joint one edge. Slowly feed the workpiece across the cutters with push blocks, applying pressure on the infeed side of the fence with your hands clear of the knives (left). Once one hand reaches the outfeed table, shift pressure to the outfeed table. Continue applying pressure just to the outfeed side of the knives until the edge is jointed, then pass the rocker through a thickness planer to clean up its other edge. Cut the ends of the rocker on the band saw.

ROCKER JOINERY

The greatest stresses in a rocking chair occur where the legs meet the rockers. These joints need to be strong and solid, otherwise the seemingly gentle act of rocking will eventually pull the chair apart. There are several effective methods for attaching legs to rockers. The simplest way is to turn a blind or through tenon in the ends of the legs and fit them into round mortises bored in the rockers *(page 134)*. The tenons can be wedged for extra strength.

Dowels *(below)* are not as sturdy as mortise-and-tenons, but they allow the legs to be trimmed to fine-tune the balance of the chair. Using bridges *(page 139)* enhances a rocking chair's appear-

Butterfly keys are one of several joinery methods used to attach rockers to a chair. Also known as a double dovetail, the butterfly key is often cut from a contrasting hardwood for decorative effect.

ance and also permit adjustment of the chair's balance. If your chair's rockers are thin, consider pinning the legs, a traditional joinery option in which the slotted legs straddle the rockers *(page 135)*. If your chair has a predominantly square look, butterfly keys *(page 137)* are strong joints that lend an attractive touch.

There is more than one way to assemble a rocking chair. If you are working from plans, you can complete the joinery on the legs and rockers before assembling the chair. But many woodworkers working on a new chair design prefer to assemble the chair first to see how it sits on the rockers before joining the legs to the rockers.

DOWELS

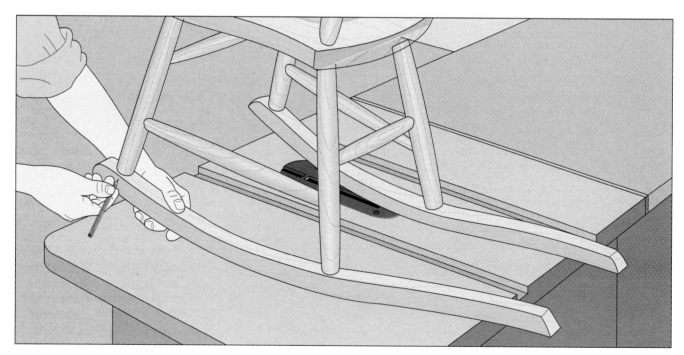

1 Balancing the chair

Align the rockers on a surface as flat as possible, such as a saw table. Then position the chair on the rockers so the back legs sit about 2 inches behind the point where the rockers contact the surface. Holding the assembly steady, gently rock the chair. It should rock smoothly with both rockers reaching the end of their forward and backward swings in unison. If the chair is pitched too far forward and will not rock back—a common problem with straight-back rockers—trim the back

legs slightly and retest. Inspect the contact point between the legs and the rockers; the legs should sit flush. If there are any gaps between the legs and rockers, sand the ends of the legs, as necessary. Once you are satisfied with the chair's balance and the fit of the legs and rockers, use a pencil to mark a line on the outside edges of the rockers directly below the center of each leg *(above)*. Transfer the lines to the tops of the rockers.

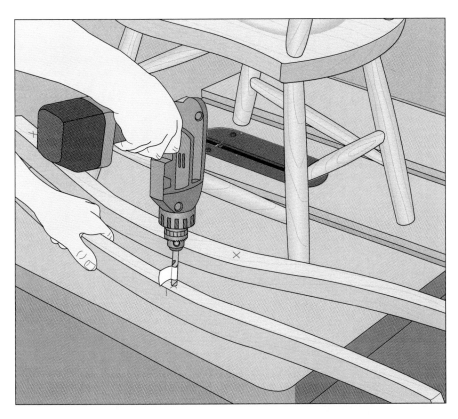

2 Drilling the dowel holes
Fit an electric drill with a bit the same diameter as the dowels you are using, and wrap a strip of masking tape around the bit to mark a drilling depth that is $\frac{1}{16}$ inch more than one-half the dowel length. Hold the rocker steady as you bore each hole *(left)*, stopping when the tape contacts the stock. Drill matching holes up through the center of each leg.

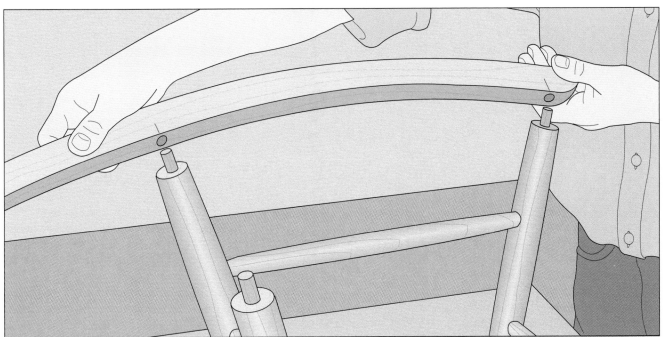

3 Installing the rockers
Set the chair upside down on a work surface and use a stick to dab a small amount of glue in the bottom of each dowel hole. Insert the dowels into the legs, using a wooden mallet to tap them into position. Then fit the rockers in place *(above)*, using the mallet with a wood striking block to tap the rockers flush with the legs. Clamp the joints until the glue is cured.

WEDGED TENONS

1 Drilling holes for the tenons

If you are using wedged tenons to join the legs to the rockers, you will need to turn a tenon at the bottom of each leg as you would on a stretcher *(page 104)*. For a through tenon, make the tenon equal in length to the height of the rockers; for a blind tenon, make it one-half as long. Mark the location of the legs on the rockers *(page 132)*, then install a bit in your drill press the same diameter as the tenon. To bore each hole, set the rocker on a scrap panel on the machine table, align the leg mark under the bit, and clamp the rocker in place, using a shim to hold the workpiece flat *(right)*. Drill the hole completely through the rocker for a through tenon or $\frac{1}{16}$ inch past the halfway point for a blind tenon.

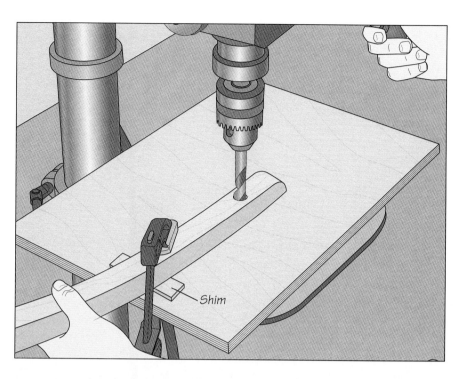

Shim

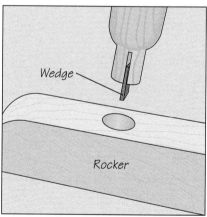

Wedge

Rocker

3 Joining the legs to the rockers

Insert the wedges into their kerfs, then apply glue to the tenons and in their holes. Set the rockers on a work surface, then seat the legs into position *(above)*. Tap the rockers and legs together with a mallet and a striking block; the wedges will push the tenons tightly against the insides of the holes. If you are using through tenons, insert the leg in the rocker and hammer the wedge in place from the bottom. Clamp the joints until the glue cures.

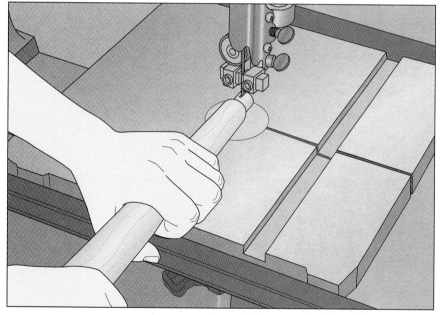

2 Kerfing the legs for the wedges

To prepare each leg for a wedge, hold the leg flat on your band saw table, aligning the middle of the tenon with the blade. Position the leg so the kerf—and the wedge—will be perpendicular to the grain of the rocker. Feed the stock into the blade *(above)*, stopping the cut about ¼ inch from the tenon shoulder. Cut the wedges from a dense hardwood slightly thicker than the kerfs. Make sure the grain of the wedges runs lengthwise, rather than across their width.

PINNED LEGS

1 **Notching the legs**
If you choose to pin the legs to the rockers, prepare the legs before gluing up the chair. You can notch the legs quickly and accurately with a commercial tenoning jig on your table saw. The model at right slides in the miter slot. Outline a notch on the bottom end of each leg, making its width equal to the thickess of the rockers. Set the cutting height to about one-half the height of the rockers and, using a wood pad to protect the stock, clamp the leg end-up in the jig. Adjust the jig sideways to align one of the notch marks with the blade. Make the first cut by pushing the jig forward, feeding the leg into the blade, then turn the leg around to cut the other side of the notch. To clear the waste between the two cuts, adjust the jig sideways and make as many passes as necessary *(right)*. If you will be turning the legs, mark the center of the notch *(step 2)*; otherwise, prepare the legs for pinning *(step 3)*.

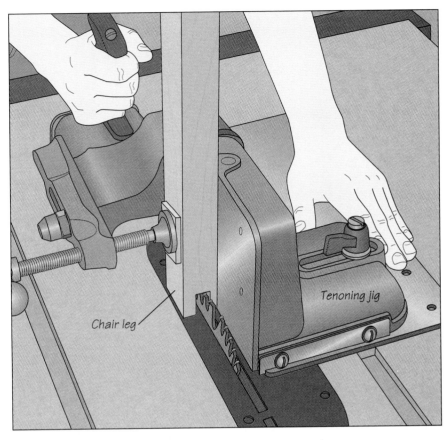

Chair leg

Tenoning jig

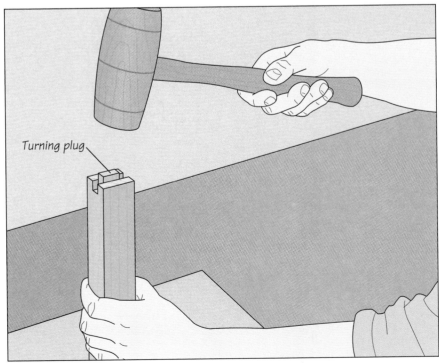

Turning plug

2 **Preparing the legs for turning**
To mount the legs on your lathe, you need to provide the drive center in the headstock or tailstock with a solid surface to butt against at the notched end. Cut a wood plug for each leg slightly thicker than the width of the notch. Drive the plug into the notch with a wooden mallet *(left)*, then turn the leg *(page 102)*.

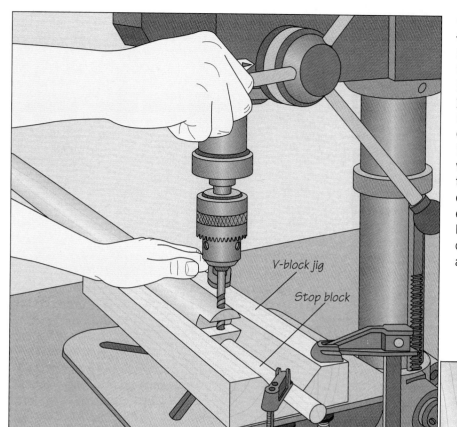

V-block jig

Stop block

3 Preparing the legs for dowels

Cut a V-shaped wedge out of a wood block, creating a jig that will hold the turned legs steady as your bore the dowel holes. Install a ⅜-inch brad-point bit in your drill press and clamp the jig to the machine table so the bottom of the V is centered under the bit. Then place the leg in the jig, align the middle of the notch with the bit, and clamp a length of dowel to the jig against the leg. The dowel will ensure that the holes in each leg are properly positioned. Holding the leg with one hand, bore the dowel through both sides of the notch *(left)*. Once you have prepared all four legs, glue up the chair.

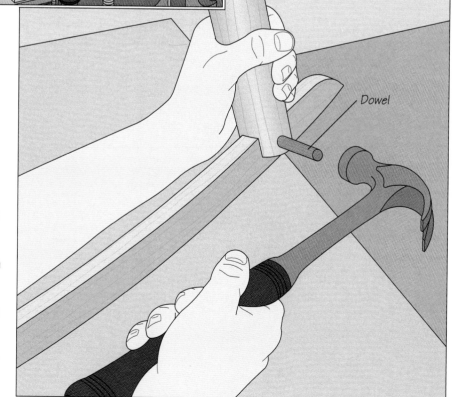

Dowel

4 Attaching the legs to the rockers

Balance the chair on the rockers *(page 132)*, then mark the matching dowel holes on the sides of the rockers, using the holes in the legs as a guide. Remove the chair and drill holes at each mark. Then reposition the chair on the rockers and cut a length of ⅜-inch dowel for each hole slightly longer than the full thickness of the legs. Spread some glue in the holes in the rockers and legs and insert the dowels, tapping each one in place with a hammer *(right)*. Pare the ends of the dowels flush using a chisel, then sand them smooth.

BUTTERFLY KEYS

1 Making the keys
If you are connecting rockers to a chair with butterfly keys, start by making the keys, using hardwood that contrasts with the leg and rocker stock. Using a ½-inch-thick strip, rip the stock ¼ inch narrower than the width of the legs. Outline two keys for each leg on the strip, making them slightly longer than the height of the rockers. Angle the sides of the keys at 10°. Once the keys are outlined, cut them from the strip on your band saw *(right)*.

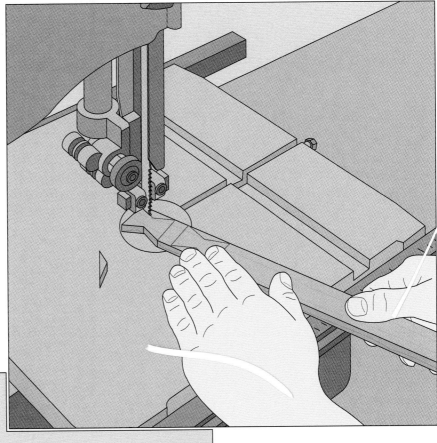

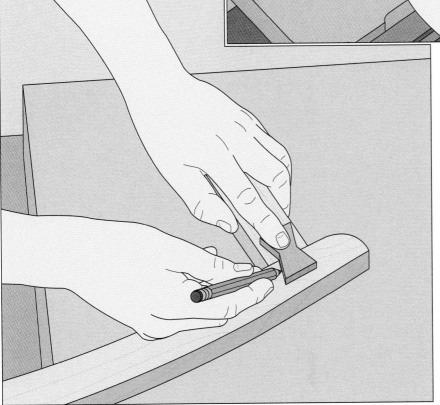

2 Outlining the recesses for the keys
If the chair has been glued up, you will need to balance it on the rockers to determine the location of the joints. In the example shown here, the chair will be assembled after the rockers and legs are joined. In either case, position the leg against the rocker, center the butterfly key on the joint and use a pencil to outline its shape on the sides of the leg and rocker *(left)*. Repeat on the other side of the joint and on both sides of the remaining legs and rockers.

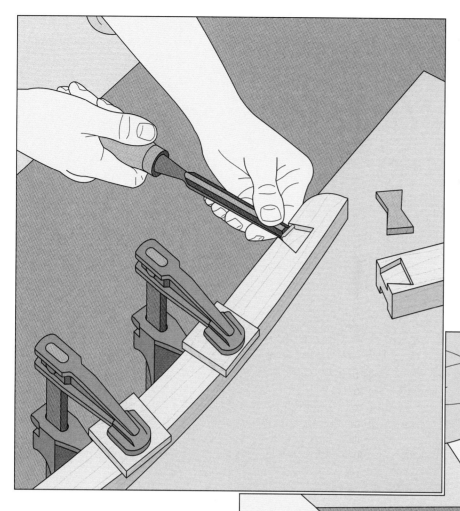

3 Making the recesses

Clamp one of the legs or rockers to a work surface, protecting the stock with wood pads. Cut the recess with a bevel-edged chisel no wider than the narrowest part of the outline. Holding the chisel horizontal, flat-side down, shave the waste wood away in thin layers *(left)*. Work carefully to cut only within the outline and to a depth slightly less than the thickness of the keys. Repeat for the remaining outlines.

4 Joining the legs and rockers

Test-fit the keys in their recesses and bevel the undersides of any that fit poorly. Then spread some glue in the recesses and insert the keys, tapping them in place with a wooden mallet *(right)*. Lay a wood pad across the panel, using clamps at its ends to hold the key in place while the glue cures. Sand the keys flush with the surface of the legs and rockers, then drive a countersunk screw from the underside of the rocker into each leg to reinforce the joint.

ADDING WOOD BRIDGES

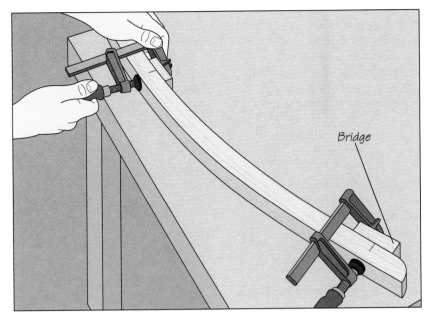

Bridge

1 Gluing the bridges to the rockers

If you are using dowels or round tenons to join the legs to the rockers, you can add bridges between the two for decorative effect and for fine-tuning the balance of the chair. Mark the joints between the legs and rockers *(page 132)*, then glue a bridge to the top edge of the rockers at each mark *(above)*. Cut the bridges to the same width as the rockers and about one-half as thick from the stock used to build the chair. If the rockers are laminated, you can use the same technique to make the bridges.

2 Shaping the bridges

Once the glue securing the bridges has cured, reposition the chair on the rockers and use a pencil to mark curves on each bridge near the ends to enhance the visual flow from rocker to leg *(above)*. Cut away the waste on the band saw.

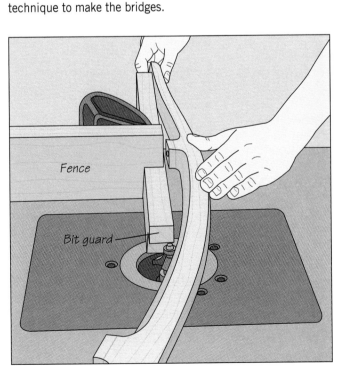

Fence

Bit guard

3 Rounding over the edges of the rockers

To further enhance the visual appeal of the rockers, round over their top edges. Install a ½-inch piloted round-over bit in a router and mount the tool in a table. To provide a bearing surface for the rockers, fashion a guard for the bit and a fence for the stock to ride against the infeed side of the table. Screw the guard and fence together and clamp them to the table. Press the workpiece against the pilot bearing as you feed each rocker across the table, then turn over the stock and rout the other edge *(left)*. Use a push stick to complete each pass. Once both rockers have been rounded over, attach them to the legs. Then use a rasp to smooth the joint and form a seamless transition between the bridges and the legs *(photo, page 124)*.

GLOSSARY

A-B-C

Air-dried wood: Lumber that has been dried to a specific moisture content by exposure to the air; see *kiln-dried wood*.

Angled tenon: A tenon sawn at an angle to the edges and ends of the workpiece; typically cut at the ends of the side rails of a frame chair that is wider at the front than at the back.

Back rail: A horizontal frame piece near the bottom of a chair back; joined to the rear legs with tenons. See *crest rail*.

Bead: A rounded, convex shape cut in wood, usually for decoration.

Blank: A piece of solid or glued-up lumber used to create a chair part, such as a turned leg.

Blind tenon: A tenon that is completely hidden in the mortise workpiece; see *through tenon*.

Brad-point bit: A drill bit featuring a sharpened centerpoint and two cutting spurs on its circumference; produces cleaner holes than a twist bit.

Butterfly key joint: A butt joint reinforced by a wing-shaped key that is often made of a contrasting hardwood for decorative effect; typically used to join the rockers to the legs of a rocking chair.

Cabriole leg: A type of leg characterized by rounded contours designed to imitate the graceful leg of a leaping animal.

Cane: The outer bark of the rattan plant; strands of this strong, flexible material can be woven into chair seats and backs.

Corner block: Triangular wood blocks screwed to the inside corners of a frame chair's seat rails to strengthen the chair and support a drop-in seat.

Countersink: To drill a hole so the head of a screw will lie flush with or slightly below the wood surface.

Cove: A rounded, concave decorative profile cut in wood.

Crest rail: A horizontal frame piece at the top of a chair back; tenons at its ends join the rail to the rear legs. See *back rail*.

Crosscut: A saw cut made across the grain of a workpiece.

Cutting list: A list of lumber pieces in the sizes needed for a furniture project.

D-E-F-G-H-I

Dowel joint: A butt joint reinforced and aligned by dowels.

Ergonomics: The science of measuring and fitting the human anatomy to furniture design.

Face gluing: Bonding several boards together face to face to form a thicker workpiece.

Fairing: Shaping and smoothing a joint between curved chair parts, usually with a rasp.

Featherboard: A piece of wood with thin, springy "fingers" at one end; used in conjunction with clamps to hold a workpiece secure against the fence or table of a power tool.

Fence: An adjustable guide designed to keep the edge or face of a workpiece a fixed distance from the cutting edge of a tool.

Frame chair: A chair made of legs and rails to which a seat is attached; the seat adds no structural strength to the chair (*see slab-and-stick chair*).

French curve: A marking tool used to draw curved lines.

Grain: The arrangement and direction of the fibers that make up wood.

Green wood: Freshly felled, unseasoned wood with its fibers still saturated by moisture.

Groove: A rectangular cut along the grain of a workpiece.

Half-lap joint: A joint in which both mating boards are dadoed to one-half the thickness of the stock, allowing the surfaces of the pieces to lie flush with one another when the joint is assembled.

J-K-L-M-N-O-P-Q

Jig: A device for guiding a tool or holding a workpiece in position.

Kerf: The cut in a workpiece made by a saw blade.

Kerfed tenon: A tenon in which a saw cut is made lengthwise to accept a wedge.

Kiln-dried wood: Lumber that has been oven-dried to a specific moisture content; see *air-dried wood*.

Ladder-back chair: A type of stick chair with a back made up of horizontal rows of slats mortised into the back posts.

Lumbar region: The lower five vertebrae of the spine, also known as the small of the back; requires the most support by a chair.

Mortise: A rectangular, round, or oval hole cut into a piece of wood to receive a matching tenon.

Mortise-and-tenon joint: A joinery technique in which a tenon on one board fits into a mortise in another.

Nominal size: The dimensions to which lumber is sawn before drying or planing; wood is sold according to nominal size.

Pilot bearing: A cylindrical metal collar either above or below the router bit's cutting edge that rides along the workpiece or a template, guiding the workpiece during a cut.

Platform: A wooden bridge positioned between the legs and rockers of a rocking chair; used to fine-tune the chair's balance.

Pommel: A rounded shoulder produced on the lathe; serves to separate square and cylindrical sections of a leg.

Post: The vertical members of a slab-and-stick chair's back assembly.

Push stick: A device used to feed a workpiece into the blade or bit of a tool to protect the operator's fingers.

R-S

Rail: A horizontal frame joined to the legs of a frame chair by mortise-and-tenon joints; supports the chair seat in a frame chair.

Rake angle: The angle at which a chair leg or post deviates from the vertical when viewed from the side of the chair.

Resawing: Ripping a large board into narrower pieces, often for laminate bending.

Rip cut: A saw cut that follows the grain of a workpiece—usually made along its length.

Riving: The technique of splitting wood from a freshly felled log with a sledgehammer and wedges to separate the wood along the fibers.

Rocker: The curved runners of a rocking chair joined to the chair legs; can be laminated from strips of resawn stock or band sawn from a solid piece of wood.

Rung: A turned spindle joining and reinforcing the legs of a stool or chair.

Rush: A natural fiber made from the twisted leaves of cattails used for seating material in stick chairs.

Seasoning: The process or technique of drying wood.

Slab-and-stick chair: A chair in which the legs and back posts are joined directly to the seat, which provides integral support to the chair *(see frame chair)*.

Slat: A vertical member in a chair back assembly between the rear legs or posts, often turned and mortised into the back and crest rails; also known as a mullion.

Sliding bevel: A measuring and marking tool used to measure the angle between two adjoining workpieces or the fence and table of a stationary power tool.

Splay angle: The angle at which a chair leg or post deviates from the vertical when viewed from the front of the chair.

Spline: A wedge-shaped piece of reeding from the core of the rattan palm; used to anchor prewoven cane in a groove in a chair seat or back.

Steam bending: The technique of softening wood for bending by subjecting it to steam and heat and then bending it around a curved form.

T-U-V-W-X-Y-Z

Template: A pattern cut from plywood, hardwood, or particleboard to produce multiple copies of a chair part.

Tenon: A projecting member on the end of a workpiece; fits into a mortise.

Through tenon: A tenon that passes completely through the mortise piece; see *blind tenon*.

Wedged tenon: A tenon that is secured by a wedge.

Windsor chair: A style of stick chair popular in the 18th Century made of a solid, sculpted seat into which the legs and back spindles are mortised; often uses steam-bent parts.

Wood movement: The shrinkage or swelling of wood in reaction to changes in humidity.

INDEX

Page references in *italics* indicate an illustration of subject matter. Page references in **bold** indicate a Build It Yourself project.

ACKNOWLEDGMENTS

The editors wish to thank the following:

CHAIR-BUILDING BASICS
Michael Fortune, Toronto, Ont.; Carolyn and John Grew-Sheridan,
San Francisco, CA; Drew Langsner, Marshall, NC

FRAME CHAIRS
Adjustable Clamp Co., Chicago, IL; American Tools Cos., Lincoln, NE; Black and Decker/Elu Power Tools, Hunt Valley, MD;
Delta International Machinery/Porter Cable, Guelph, Ont.; Freud Westmore Tools, Mississauga, Ont.; General Tools Manufacturing
Co., New York, NY; Lee Valley Tools Ltd., Ottawa, Ont.; Ryobi America Corp., Anderson, SC; Tool Trend, Concord, Ont.

SLAB-AND-STICK CHAIRS
Adjustable Clamp Co., Chicago, IL; American Tools Cos., Lincoln, NE; Black and Decker/Elu Power Tools, Hunt Valley, MD;
Delta International Machinery/Porter Cable, Guelph, Ont.; Mike Dunbar, Portsmouth, NH; Lee Valley Tools Ltd.,
Ottawa, Ont.; Sandvik Saws and Tools Co., Scranton, PA; Stanley Tools, Division of the Stanley Works, New Britain, CT;
Tool Trend, Concord, Ont.; The Woodworkers Store, Rogers, MN

SEATS
Adjustable Clamp Co., Chicago, IL; American Tools Cos., Lincoln, NE; Delta International Machinery/Porter Cable,
Guelph, Ont.; Great Neck Saw Mfrs. Inc. (Buck Bros. Division), Millbury, MA; H.H. Perkins, Woodbridge, CT;
Intermares Trading Co., Lindenhurst, NY; Lee Valley Tools Ltd., Ottawa, Ont.; Tool Trend, Concord, Ont.

LEGS AND STRETCHERS
Adjustable Clamp Co., Chicago, IL; Delta International Machinery/Porter Cable, Guelph, Ont.; Record Tools Inc., Pickering, Ont.;
Sears, Roebuck and Co., Chicago, IL; Woodcraft Supply Corp., Parkersburg, WV; Woodturner's World, Gabriola, B.C.

ARMS AND BACKS
Adjustable Clamp Co., Chicago, IL; American Tools Cos., Lincoln, NE; Delta International Machinery/Porter Cable,
Guelph, Ont.; Great Neck Saw Mfrs. Inc. (Buck Bros. Division), Millbury, MA; H.H. Perkins, Woodbridge, CT;
Intermares Trading Co., Lindenhurst, NY; Lee Valley Tools Ltd., Ottawa, Ont.; Tool Trend, Concord, Ont.

ROCKING CHAIRS
Adjustable Clamp Co., Chicago, IL; Delta International Machinery/Porter Cable, Guelph, Ont.;
Lee Valley Tools Ltd., Ottawa, Ont.; Sam Maloof, Alta Loma, CA; Ryobi America Corp., Anderson, SC;
Sears, Roebuck and Co., Chicago, IL; Tool Trend, Concord, Ont.

The following persons also assisted in the preparation of this book:
Art Chesmer, Lorraine Doré, Alan Flegg, Graphor Consultation, Solange Laberge, Geneviève Monette

---

PICTURE CREDITS

Cover Robert Chartier
6,7 Gary Moss
8,9 Steve Lewis
10,11 Sharon Beals
12 Martin Fox
13 Sharon Beals
18 Michael C. Fortune Studio
125 Gary Moss